658.564
K64B

Blackburn College-Lumpkin Library
0 00 51 0009367 2

D1608836

BOXED AND LABELLED

NEW APPROACHES TO PACKAGING DESIGN

gestalten

CONTENT

IN A NUTSHELL

In the beginning, humans didn't need packaging. They had gourds, shells and leaves, hollow logs or bark, baskets, animal organs, wineskins and amphorae. But as they moved away from hunting and gathering to agriculture and mercantilism, traders needed to store and transport their merchandise; measure it out in equal amounts for comparable pricing; protect it from contamination and theft; and, as exports travelled beyond the region of manufacture, a way to make their products – and companies – appear recognisable and reliable. The solution? Packaging. The first trademark adorned a relatively simple glass jar of English cough drops in 1866; by the mid-20th century, however, the overdesign of packaging had become rampant. Products began to shout each other down across the aisles of supermarkets – and the cacophony of overconsumption had begun.

POWER TO THE PEOPLE

At the outset of the 21st century, the design of new commercial packaging is increasingly shaped by international and national trade decisions. The European Union, for example, decided to lift packaging regulations instead of trying to synchronise standards across its 27 member nations. This encourages competition and innovation in design certainly, but such a plethora of sizes, shapes and costs for similar products may also create confusion amongst shoppers. Fortunately, today's consumer is more educated and powerful than ever. With access to the Internet, shoppers can research products and tap into forums and discussions to compare notes. As Chris Zawada, founder of Canadian blog Lovely Packaging, puts it: "No longer is just having an eye-catching and compelling package enough to convince people to buy your product." And yet, design can have a massive impact on sales. "When we're doing a client's packaging, we're branding for them," explains Leif Steiner, owner of graphic design agency Moxie Sozo from Boulder, Colorado, which repackaged a fruit-and-nut-bar, increasing its baseline sales seven-fold. The client had to dump thousands bars in the old wrappers because they weren't selling anymore. "Every time we've done a client's packaging, it hasn't been: Can they afford to do a redesign?" says Steiner. "It's been: How can they afford to not do a redesign?"

WANT IT, DON'T WASTE IT

As climate change rocks the world, it is also rocking the design world. "At this point in the history of industry, those who integrate environmentally friendly solutions into their practice will be in demand," warns design professor Sylvain Allard of the University of Quebec at Montreal (UQAM). "Those who resist will simply be pushed out of the market."

The pressure on companies to go green comes not just from the consumers, but also from up and down the supply chain and, not least, from their own bookkeepers. Packaging has been an obvious place to begin. Germans now leave packaging at the supermarket to be recycled, which means that supermarkets, in turn, put pressure on producers to reduce their packaging. In the UK, shoppers can bring their own boxes to buy cereal, and almost everywhere, there is a move from bottled water to tap, not just in homes and restaurants, but hotels.

There are many shades of green, from "Reduce, Reuse, Recycle" to making the best of what you've inherited and then passing it down to the next generation. "I think the biggest consumer misconception in this area is that for packaging to be sustainable, it has to be minimal," says Lovely Packaging's Chris Zawada. "But this isn't the case. The companies doing it right are sourcing local packaging facilities, using local production and dissecting every step in their process to see how to reduce their carbon footprint."

Another misconception? Although plastic has been widely vilified, most designers know that it is more important to decrease the amount of material used than to get rid of polymers altogether. Sure, the calculus – local plastic vs. imported paper – can get confusing. And because green has gone mainstream only recently, a lot of companies are "greenwashing" to sell more products, in much the same way that 17th-century English merchants sold inferior merchandise to a naïve public, inspiring the first officially trademarked product. "But we're also seeing a genuine shift," suggests Moxie Sozo's Steiner. "Whereas before companies said, 'Make this look green,' they are now actually trying to make it green because they understand that that will translate into sales." Steiner –, who runs a carbon-neutral, renewable-energy-powered, zero-waste studio, with a compost bin in the alley out the back – works with printers who use wind power, among other things and is sought out by clients precisely for this walk-the-talk approach. He has watched the transition toward less material (hang tags instead of boxes, for instance), bio-based, biodegradable and recyclable materials and packaging that serves multiple purposes. In part, the trend is being

deepened by global economic woes: "A lot of great products and innovation have come out of smaller budgets and economic downturns because clients demand more effective solutions," Steiner says. "When the economy slows down, it shakes a lot of fossils loose."

Sometimes, responsible packaging design is as simple as making a wrapper that the consumer wants to live with. Designers are building a second life into their packaging, giving an additional function to the container: an emptied wine box becomes a wine rack, a perfume bottle can be used as a travel case. A shoebox is used to store love letters or even the shoes, themselves. Sometimes this reuse is brief, but sometimes the box enjoys a longer "product" life than the product does. "In the near future, packaging may be re-purposed in different ways after it is used: converted into a game, a container, a message, furniture and so on," says Portland-based designer Chean Wei Law, aka undoboy, who has made game and music packaging. "People collect things, so beautiful, conceptual design generates enough extra value that people keep it and take pride in it."

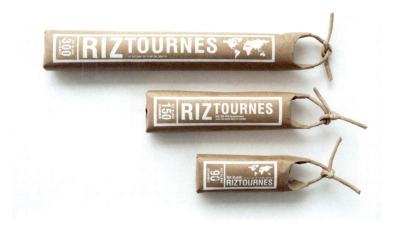

BREAKING DOWN THE BOX

So what's the difference between packaging and prodigality? Designers'toolkits include a variety of three-dimensional (shape, material, construction) and two-dimensional elements (label, typography, illustration, colour, pattern) to soften the hard-sell, and to bridge the advertising, shopping and post-purchase experiences of both products and brands. "Our job is to create a little voice on the shelf, when the consumer walks by, that winks at them to stand out among thousands of screaming voices," says Steiner. The most strategically packaged goods are gratuitous purchases, like chocolate or tea. Staple products, like eggs, are a more rational purchase; chocolate needs sex appeal. It doesn't need to speak to everyone walking by, but it needs to send out a siren call to a handful.

Standing in front of a shelf of the same product in different packing, a shopper will usually get a quick read (accurate or not) of which is the most or least valuable version. Packaging sometimes takes advantage of deeply held associations to hook buyers, using familiar wrappers that correspond with a particular but very different type of product – "candy cigarettes" are sticks of gum in a pack of smokes. This approach can be benign or manipulative, but it generates a sense of "gilt by association" that can spark the compulsive buy. Sometimes reverse psychology will do the trick, as well: even low-cost products boast more sophisticated package design today (like IKEA Food by Stockholm Design Lab), while some of the most expensive products (organic food, for instance) opt for a humble wrapper and handwritten labels to underscore the authenticity of the product.

Via, GS1 and Natcoll are turning the bars into flower stems topped with blossoms, or into oil paint oozing out of its tube. In Japan, barcodes depict anything from noodles draped over chopsticks, a waterfall or rain on an umbrella to a gun, a skyline or a surfer in the pipeline of a monster wave.

Simplicity of design can be a merciful acknowledgement of today's widespread information overload or, conversely, an effort to generate more of it: "As computing power expanded in the last decade, we were faced with an onslaught of high-tech, 3D graphics," suggests Base Design New York partner Geoff Cook. "Now, perhaps in reaction to this trend, graphics are trending toward greater simplicity. With the web and various mobile devices becoming an increasingly important part of marketing and branding strategies, packaging design will be approached in an increasingly systematic way because its design elements must also be applied to motion graphics."

At other times, minimalism is used to express the pedigree or individuality of a product. Luxury packaging often differs from the mass-market by cultivating a covetous unapproachability. Berlin's Humeicki & Graef fragrances communicate their luxury through austerity. The naked rectangular bottles have an astringent but sensual economy. "The simplicity of the design should keep the focus on the most important thing, the fragrance," says H&G co-founder Sebastian Fischenich. "A perfume flacon is just packaging, a 'reliquiar' for a very exceptional creation. This should be celebrated and not obscured by unnecessary design."

But what about necessary design that proves distracting? Usually considered the ugly duckling of packaging, barcodes – unavoidable, insipid, useful – are being transformed. Mexican Tecate beer features a barcode in the shape of a spread-winged eagle. In New Zealand,

THE GLO-BAL STORY IS LOCAL

Barcodes, like many products, are international, but the way designers treat them must function at the local level. Even Coca-Cola, which sells in every corner of the globe (to judge by the litter), prints regional versions of its cans. Packing must respond to local interpretations of colour and symbol, not just language. Cleaning liquids and washing powders in Europe are often boxed in vivid greens or lemon-yellow (signs of freshness) while in the US, they tend to feature brightly aggressive colours like Tide's safety orange (the sign of heavy-duty strength). Brands in the US, where weddings are white, must use the colour in considered ways in Japan, since white is associated with death there. Designers must honour and exploit these cultural differences in order to avoid international incidents.

TIME IS SUBJECTIVE

Like brand logos, packaging has evolved from the historical permanence of a single design to a medium that is often updated. Today, companies want specialized packaging and regular updates to be a part of the product design, as a whole. Once upon a time, all Nike sneakers left the shops in the same orange box; today, the company puts out regular small collections and special editions. Certainly, there are products that require a fresh label periodically: wines must indicate a difference in content from year to year, fashions – colours, cuts, themes – change seasonally. Other products don't require such a frequent change of costume. In fact, some venerable old institutions, like fashion house Hermès, may change their products regularly but have hardly touched their historical packaging at all, letting this longevity declare the aristocracy of the product and brand. Other companies, laundry detergents or juices might not change their product at all over time, but need, nonetheless, to persuade the customer to choose their brand repeatedly by telling them a fresh story with relative frequency.

A (LESS AND LESS) MATERIAL WORLD

As the developing world booms, the volume of packaging will boom and the need for concrete solutions to waste will become, more than ever, a priority. "If recycling is now accepted as a key to environmental concerns, recycled material will need to be fully integrated in the production of new packaging for it to become a long-term sustainable solution," UQAM's Prof. Allard explains.

To expedite the recycling process, the one-material package may become standard even while the materials palette expands. In the next decade, bioplastics like palm and reed fibre and bamboo (PLAs) may begin to replace more profligate materials. Education will be crucial to making them sustainable, however, since they can pose a major problem if mixed with standard plastics during the recycling process. Bioplastics could prove particularly helpful where recycling is difficult (like the US) because biopolymers revert back to organic material when composted correctly. They are durable, easy to print on and have a pleasant texture and anti-static properties. Researchers are also looking into making thinner, multilayer barrier-PET, as well as chemical barriers that will eliminate the need for sealed plastic packages. Meanwhile, additives are being explored that could break down discarded plastics more quickly.

Because the cost of raw materials has increased globally, according to Simon Farrow of Progress Packaging in the UK, he is constantly on the lookout for more cost-effective solutions. Progress prefers vegetable-based inks, biodegradable laminates and traceably green raw materials. At the moment, these products cost a premium, but as demand increases, Farrow says, the price will fall precipitously.

SMART PACKAGING: THE FUTURE?

Today, college kids have got their self-cooling beer kegs while office workers have their self-heating coffee cups, but smart packaging – once pie in the sky – is nearly ready for retail. "In the next ten years," anticipates Allard, "packaging design will include nanotechnology in many applications: for tamper evidence and pack integrity, safety and quality, traceability and product authenticity."

Indeed, in the near future, packaging may be nanomechanical, biogenetic, audible (in fact nearly cinematic) and capable of responding to environmental stressors like pH value, temperature or pressure – even breaches of security. According to British trend forecasters The Future Laboratory, scientists are developing lightweight and invisible coatings or embedded particles, nano-materials, nanotubes and nanofillers, that could detect pathogens or delay food spoilage by putting up oxygen barriers or catalysing chemical reactions. Bizerba has developed a sticker for food labels that changes colour with changes in temperature: If a product requiring refrigeration during shipping arrives at its destination above a certain temperature, the supplier, merchant or consumer would be immediately aware of the fact. Radio-Frequency Identification chips could tell homeowners when items in their refrigerator approach or pass their expiration dates. Integrated into packaging, RFID and near field communications could even interface with mobile phones, creating new efficiency in shopping. Forget the movie theatre: consumers can look forward to a time when – using moving on-pack graphics, small, flexible OLED displays that play video clips and animation, and printed electronics that can communicate with point-of-purchase displays – products on the shelves will be just as vociferous as ever, but among them there will be those that giggle, others that hum, and even a growing handful that will sing.

Shonquis Moreno

BASE DESIGN

Product: Store Identity
Client: BozarShop

STRIP TEASE
SWEET & SEDUCTIVE

PLAYFUL PACKAGING can be bright, pop and chock full of colour, loaded with texture, illustration, characters and animal motifs – without being freighted with nostalgia. Fluorescent shades attract young shoppers, especially to candy, energy drinks and snacks. Graphic patterns, unusual shapes and humorous imagery emphasise the novelty of the package contents, and sometimes go so far as to make the packaging itself a coveted object: Naoto Fukasawa made juice boxes with textural fruit-like skins: furry brown kiwi boxes, dimpled, seeded strawberry boxes, and rubbery banana boxes. TK COMPANY's Orange Drop Drink designed by Firm A is a puddle of coloured liquid flattened in a plastic sleeve and sipped through a straw. Designers are using fantasy illustration or forms to suggest escape and to draw buyers out of the real world and into a fantasy world – drink your juice from an oversized piece of fruit or sip it from a neon puddle of sugar water that has fallen straight from the skies of Candyland. In this approach, amorphous, un-conventional shapes, evocatively moulded plastics and even stuffed-animal plush, may be used along with eye-popping colour schemes and type that is suggestive of anything from fairyland to an imagined but very real world of wealth and opulence: The point is to make the opening of the box an experience that leaves the banal behind or below – a game, a (reusable) toy, a journey to the centre of the … wrapper. Whatever the style (and fantasy takes many forms), the journey is the destination.
At times this journey can be as puerile, sweet and superficially fantastical as Candyland; at others, it comes closer to Willy Wonka: seductively dark, irreverent, life-affirmingly morbid – even foul-mouthed. A subculture of winemakers, in particular, have been playfully transforming their labels to reach an older "child." "One of the reasons for this is that the wine market has become so oversaturated with look-a-like brands," says Chris Zawada, the Canadian founder and editor of the Lovely Package blog. "Typically these brands have a very serious, almost stagnant look and as wine appeals more and more to a younger audience, the 'old school' designs haven't retained their old appeal."

Since 2005, Australia's R Wines co-founder, Dan Philips, has been selecting designers and illustrators outside the wine industry – Alan Aldridge, Jonathan Barnbrook, Jeff Keedy and many others – to make his labels. Although buying wine is all about choice, industry pressure to conform to packaging conventions is extreme. "In general, 95% of wine packaging is a black capsule and a white label with text," laments Philips. "You can succeed in the wine business by knowing the rules and breaking them, but you need to understand the rules."

Philips believes that geometry, type and detail are crucial to bottle design. His designers play with surreal, spidery illustrations, and are unafraid to mix sky blues with bloody-nose red, print type upside down or swear gratuitously. Jeff Keedy designed a typeface for R's Bitch wine on spec. Now it's their most popular label. "If you have popular type, you're 90% of the way to a strong label," says Philips, who drafted Keedy to also do the Bitch Bubbly, Evil, Pure Evil and Evil Incarnate labels as well.

"A great package has drama," insists Philips. "We're storytellers because we're tying to convince the consumer that we're worth the price." The company's Luchador labels, featuring Mexican wrestling masks, were created by the Morning Breath studio for anyone wanting a wine to drink while watching sports. Punk Bubbles wines feature names like Stench, No Future and Rotten, that quote from that 70s subculture and go, Philips says, "directly against what champagne multinational conglomerates say it's all about: purity and luxury." Where's the fun in purity? There's got to be a little sediment in it.

ORANGE
DROP

FRUIT DRINK 0,33L

FIRMA

Product: Fruit Drops
Client: Concept / Prototype

RASPBERRY
DROP

10 \

FRUIT DRINK 0,33L

PETER KAO

Product: Gloji
Client: Gloji
Material: Glass

The idea of the Gloji package design is based on three related elements: first, the brand name "GLOJI", second, the main ingredient "Goji berry juice", and third, the slogan "The juice that makes you glow". By using a lightbulb-shaped bottle, it visually communicates the ideas of "Glowing and Healthy". In addition the bottle also represents energy, bright ideas and something that can light up your life. This innovative lightbulb shaped bottle is very ergonomic and looks and fits great in your hand.

TRUEDOT.RU

Product: Forgeron
Material: Glass, plastic

Forgeron is a farrier (from French), and the concept is for Belgian dark ale. A classic-style label is printed using silk-screen. The glass bottle form and size remind one of a big beer mug. A decorative cover looks like froth. The appearance says: "The beer's just been poured and the mug is full!"

DOWLING DESIGN & ART DIRECTION

Product: Simon Patterson Colour Match Screensaver
Client: Tate Modern

Turner Prize-nominated artist Simon Patterson has created three works in his 'Colour Match' series, all with packaging designed by Dowling Design & Art Direction. The third work in the series is a screensaver featuring a recording of football commentator John Cavanagh reading football results: Pantone colours and their codes represent teams and goals. As the results are announced different Pantone colours fill the screen. The CD's packaging – a foam football held in a net bag (both ball and net in blue or red), echoes the subject matter. A booklet of instructions for installing the CD is attached to the net.

PAVEL GUBIN

Product: Sexy Tina

Erotic packaging for a milky cream liqueur named Sexy Tina. This breast-shaped bottle contains a 35% strength alcoholic drink (Irish cream). And it is highly recommended that real fans drink straight from the bottle!

HOUSE INDUSTRIES

Product: Agent Provocateur: Tweaking the Curves and Tightening the Fit
Client: Agent Provocateur
Material: Offset-printed die-cut board book with side-tie satin knickers

Book documenting the logo redesign for Agent Provocateur, a preeminent British lingerie brand.

SARAH DÉRY

Product: Ça t'a coûté un bras/
Mange ta main…
Client: All projects were developed in
a packaging class given by Professor
Sylvain Allard – Programme Director of the
Graphic Design Department at the École
de design UQAM.

The project was to design a bag that would
take a stand on the theme of consumption
and equity. Sarah's bag played on the expression "it costs you an arm (and a leg)"
and the French translated one "eat your
hand and keep other one for tomorrow".
The bag here becomes an actor and inter-
acts with the carrier in a playful way.

IMAKITA DESIGN RESEARCH INC.

Product: Paper Carrier Bag for The Crab
Client: Joy Road Inc. (Crab restaurant)
Material: Paper

The bag is designed so that the leg part can
be unfolded and spread by the employee
before a customer purchases their products,
and will flutter in the wind when carried.

Product: Paper Carrier Bag for the Chicken
Client: New Munchen Co., Lyd.
(German style restaurant)
Material: Paper

The bag is manufactured so that the beak
of the chicken will pop out.

NOBLE GRAPHICS CREATIVE STUDIO

Product: Beer Crate
Client: Carlsberg Bulgaria / Shumensko Beer
Material: Coated Paper with glossy UV polish

Through a small investment in paper bags distributed in stores, we turned pedestrians into free outdoor advertisements of "Shumensko" beer. The optical illusion of people, carrying with ease a case of beer in one hand, entertains onlookers, as well as the actual bag-owners.

RYOKO NAGAMATSU

Product: Muse Beauty Salon Shopping Bags
Client: Muse

These bags were designed as colour samples of hair extensions for distribution to visitors at a party at Muse Beauty Salon. Hair extensions are attached to bags as handles.

OGILVY & MATHER HONG KONG

Product: Panadol Extra
Client: GlaxoSmithKline / Panadol

Punch / Tear / Stir – these give away souvenirs are distributed from pharmacies to the public to remind them that Panadol Extra can effectively remedy different types of pain for sufferers.

Product: Store Identity
Client: BozarShop

Product: Stop'n'Grow
Client: Stop'n'Grow

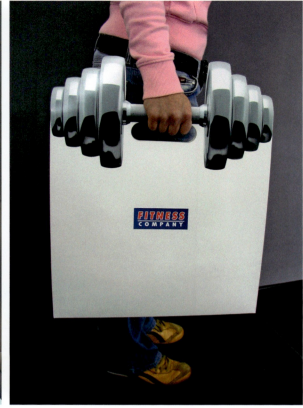

TBWA\ISTANBUL

Product: Shopping Bags
Client: YKM
Material: Cardboard, rope

We placed the figure of a man and a woman who are using a skipping rope on shopping bags. The handle of the bags formed the skipping rope.

PUBLICIS FRANKFURT GMBH

Product: Hand Weight
Client: Fitness First Germany GmbH
Material: Kraft paper

This shopping bag was given away to customers when purchasing fitness accessories or nutritional supplements at the fitness centre. Through an eye-deceiving style of hand weight, the bag created a buzz by a successful word of mouth promotion. Customers asked for the bag at the Fitness Centre and enjoyed strolling along the city centre's streets with it.

TBWA \ ISTANBUL

Product: Healthy Tea Bags
Client: House Cafe Istanbul
Material: Paper

We placed cut-out images of people doing outdoor sports on strings of herbal tea bags. The tea was served in mugs with these images on them.

OGILVY & MATHER HONG KONG

Product: Panadol Extra
Client: GlaxoSmithKline / Panadol

VITULA'S PICKLES

KAD - KYM ABRAMS DESIGN

Product: Vitula's Pickles
Client: Vitula's Pickles
Material: Cut label

This secret recipe was handed down through generations from
great Auntie Vitula. Vitula's special touch was to add grape leaves
from her very own backyard to each hand-assembled jar of pickles.
Today the pickles are hand picked each season, along the lakeside
of Michigan. Each jar is still carefully hand packed, and shipped to
a select group of family, friends, and customers.

LIGHTHOUSE STUDIO

Product: Quick Fruit
Client: Personal Project/LightHouse Studio

The idea behind Quick Fruit packaging is a fruit sliced in half showing the core of the fruit as the lid of.

DOWLING DESIGN & ART DIRECTION

Product: John Lewis Childrenswear
Client: John Lewis Partnership

We have been on the John Lewis design roster for a number of years, designing a variety of packaging for lines including lighting, gardening and bathroom accessories. For Childrenswear we used illustration as a way of engaging the audience, devising different characters for boys and girls that worked across many different age groups. The scheme included packaging, ticketing, woven labels, care labels and size stickers for John Lewis own-brand range of clothing and accessories.

PENTAGRAM DESIGN LIMITED

Product: Packaging for a new natural, no-calorie sweetener
Client: Truvia

CARACAS

Product: Fruit Juices
Client: Jean-Louis Bissaron

DESIGNKONTORET SILVER

Product: Packaging Design ICA Juice
Client: ICA AB

**TURNER DUCKWORTH:
LONDON & SAN FRANCISCO**

Product: Coca-Cola Summer 2009 Packaging
Client: The Coca-Cola Company

ROSENSTAND & CO

Product: Organa (Carbonated Organic Softdrink)
Client: House of Beer

**TURNER DUCKWORTH:
LONDON & SAN FRANCISCO**

Product: Bootleg
Client: Click Wine Group

TDA ADVERTISING & DESIGN

Product: Izze Beverage Company
Client: Izze Beverage Company

ENORMOUSCHAMPION

Product: The Kingdom Animalia
Client: Enormouschampion
Material: Recycled paper and cardboard

The colour boxes coordinate with the wooden animal silhouette they contain. Made with 2-ply recycled cardboard, the rigid boxes are intended to complement the animal silhouette and be kept as a durable container.

CLARA EZCURRA & MARÍA OLASCOAGA

Product: Herbs & Spices
Client: 1854
Material: Tins with metallised labels made of silver foil paper

40cc tins for 1854 herbs & spices.

SCHNEITER MEIER KÜLLING AG

<u>Product:</u> Migros Sélection Demi-homard
<u>Client:</u> Migros
<u>Material:</u> Card Box

SCHNEITER MEIER KÜLLING AG

<u>Product:</u> Migros Sélection Viande Séchée de Cerf
<u>Client:</u> Migros
<u>Material:</u> Carton

SCHNEITER MEIER KÜLLING AG

<u>Product:</u> Migros Sélection 70% Cacao de Venezuela
<u>Client:</u> Migros
<u>Material:</u> Card Box

SCHNEITER MEIER KÜLLING AG

<u>Product:</u> Migros Sélection Persiensalz
<u>Client:</u> Migros
<u>Material:</u> Card Box

The red rice grain is the seed of an aquatic grass, which grows wild in the rice fields. When the main rice crop was harvested the red rice was removed and thrown away. However, one day a curious farmer decided to cook the red rice. He liked the flavour so much he started to cultivate it as a crop.

The rice fields in Piedmont are home to many species of wildlife including the heron. Great care is taken in the cultivation of the rice to protect the habitat of this magnificent bird.

COOKING INSTRUCTIONS

Red rice has a nutty texture. It is a wholegrain rice, therefore takes longer to cook than other varieties of rice. Bring a large pan of water to the boil. Add a large pinch of salt then the rice and cook for approximately 40 minutes. Drain the water. It is then best served sautéed with chicken or fish or served in a salad.

RISO DI AIRONI

Carluccio's

Riso Rosso Selvatico

WILD RED RICE

500 g ℮

TRINIDAD
el chocolate
BITTER SWEET 74 %
cacao mass
CHOCOLATE

IRVING

Product: Riso Rosso Selvatico
Client: Carluccio's
Material: Carton and uncoated self adhesive label

TRINIDAD
el chocolate
MILK 40 %
cacao mass
CHOCOLATE

TRINIDAD
el chocolate
pistachio
BITTER SWEET 70 %
cacao mass
CHOCOLATE

TRINIDAD
el chocolate
almond
BITTER SWEET 70 %
cacao mass
CHOCOLATE

BLEND-IT

Product: Chocolate Store
Client: Trinidad

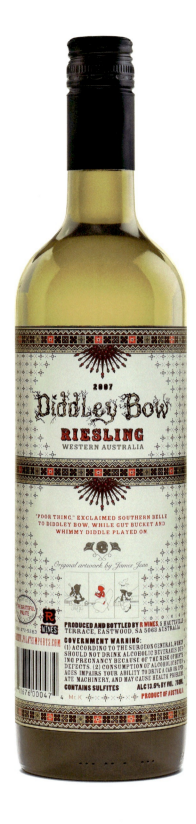

JAMES JEAN, MR. KEEDY

Product: Diddley Bow Riesling
Client: R Wines
Material: Glass and paper

Southern "gut bucket" blues served as the inspiration for "Diddley Bow" Riesling. The story unfolds across three panels (one per bottle), each conceived and illustrated by artist James Jean. Designer Mr. Keedy framed the imagery with distinctive, foil-flecked, Southern inspired ornamentation and typography. The bottles are available individually or as a triptych set.

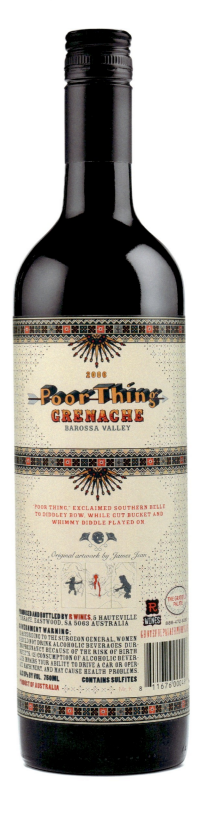

JAMES JEAN, MR. KEEDY

Product: Poor Thing Grenache
Client: R Wines
Material: Glass and paper

Weeping oak trees draped with iconic
Southern kudzu vines are the backdrop of
a sad romance of angel, cupid and hunter.

DESIGNERS JOURNEY

Product: As it Should Be, Claremont Traminer Riesling, Claremont Shiraz
Client: Arcus As

DESIGNERS JOURNEY

Product: A la Petite Ferme
Client: Arcus As
Material: Cardboard

BIG FISH DESIGN LTD

Product: Vodka and Gin
Client: Sipsmith

A STRANGE MATTER

Product: Motley Bird
Client: Kama Beverages SA
Material: Aluminium

PEARLFISHER

Product: Green & Spring
Client: A Curious Group Of Hotels

DAVID FUNG ONLINE

Product: Two Owls Premium Lager Beer
Bottle
Client: Two Owls Premium Lager

KIMO OUELLETTE

Client: This project was developed in a packaging class given by Professor Sylvain Allard – Programme Director of the Graphic Design Department at the École de design UQAM.

Sylvain Allard: "Not all the bear bottles have twist caps and if they do, it can hurt your hand after 10 or 20. (Yes we drink a lot of beer in Quebec and especially in the Saguenay region.) In my packaging class, Kimo thought of that with a four pack that includes a bottle opener that can be kept for camping or any outdoor activities."

TURNER DUCKWORTH:
LONDON & SAN FRANCISCO

Product: Oakville Grocery
Client: Oakville Grocery

MY CUP OF TEA (UK) LTD

Product: My Cup of Tea
Client: My Cup of Tea (UK) Ltd
Material: Strom card

LISA LLANES

Product: Perk Dog Grooming Line
Client: Perk

TDA ADVERTISING & DESIGN

Product: Bot Fortified Water
Client: Bot Fortified Water

**TURNER DUCKWORTH:
LONDON & SAN FRANCISCO**

Product: Cat Litter
Client: Waitrose Ltd

YIYING LU

Product: Nootie Pet Care Products
Client: Nootie
Material: All components recyclable plastic

CARACAS

Product: Simply Milk
Client: Orlait
Material: Carton

HATTOMONKEY

Product: Milk
Client: Molokoshka
Material: Carton

Hattomonkey has created the brand mark and packaging design for "Molokoshka" milk. The brand name is based on a combination of two Russian words: those for milk and cat. The cat is the greatest lover of milk after all, and so the main element of the packaging design is a cat that chooses the product because of its high quality.

IRVING

Product: Two by Two
Client: Artisan Biscuits
Material: Carton

LAUREN GOLEMBIEWSKI

Product: Honey Moon
Material: Glass, paper, wax, wood

Honey Moon is a promotional wine bottle that could be sent out for the first day of summer. The concept is based on the first full moon in June, which occurs near the first day of summer. It is seen as the most optimal time to harvest honey and is thus, called the honey moon. The bottle could be sent to new clients, to start the honeymoon period of a sweet new business relationship. The typeface was customized for the product.

IMAKITA DESIGN RESEARCH INC.

Product: Hanshin Tigers Wine
Client: Japan Typography Association

Whiskers are extended out on both sides of the label.

KARACTERS

Product: Silver Hills Bread
Client: Silver Hills Bakery
Material: 2 mm polyethylene with Oxobio-plast to make it bio-degradable

IRVING

Product: English Pickles for Cheese
Client: The Fine Cheese Co

UNDOBOY

Product: Little Undo
Client: Undoboy
Material: Card stock

This is an interactive candy packaging.
Each piece of packaging comes with a
toy as a surprise item.

CARLO GIOVANI

Product: Chinese Tea Box
Client: Carlo Giovani Estúdio
Material: Cardboard 250g

This is packaging and a paper toy in the same object. A beautiful chinese lady that has jasmine tea in her mouth.

HOUSE INDUSTRIES

Product: Alexander Girard Memory Game
Material: Screen printed wooden box

MOUSEGRAPHICS

Product: Spatula Putty
Client: Petrocoll S.A.
Material: Paperback

MASH

Product: Changing Lanes
Client: Viottolo
Material: Lenticular adhesive label

To tell the story behind the brand through the packaging itself. Coincidentally the two wine makers both shared the same last name, 'Lane'. Hence the brand name 'Changing Lanes'. As the bottle is tilted the face on the label changes from Mark Lane to Justin Lane (the two wine makers in question). The card they hold up also animates from 'Lane 1' to 'Lane 2'. Everything else in the image stays constant.

MORUBA

Product: Matsu
Client: Vintae

The solution adopted is faithful to Matsu's philosophy, his image has been stripped from all sorts of tricks to link directly with nature and with the people who cares about it. Thus, the Matsu's wine triology, 'El Pícaro', 'El Recio' and 'El Viejo' are represented by a portraits series of three generations that devote their lives to the field. Each one personality's embodies the characteristics of the wine that gets its name.

UNITED*

Product: Via Roma
Client: A&P

Via Roma: a brand that's not afraid to show its true personality. There are three million people in Tuscany, all different and all unique. This new authentic Italian brand shows off their true character, expression and emotion, in a way that has not been presented before in the United States. United* shot unique portraits on location for all items.

FANTASIST

Product: Mr. Burglar Whisky
Client: Mr. Burglar

The idea: I wanted to tell the real story behind the brand through the packaging itself. Thus, Mr. Burglar is born, a brand with an attractive packaging meant to highlight an intrinsic peculiarity of high quality spirits. The central element is Mr. Burglar himself, a gentleman whose style matches the essence of the brand. To further enhance the concept I used thermosensitive paper. Once buyer touches the label, their fingerprints become visible, creating a tactile connection with the product.

MASH

Product: Killibinbin Wine
Client: Killibinbin
Material: Fasson Estate 8 [Label paper stock]

The main US distributor of Killibinbin wines was always commenting on these wines as being 'Killer'. A tongue-in-cheek approach and a play on words lead to the final idea, taking this 'Killer' comment as the theme for re-packaging the Killibinbin wines. Illustrations were developed, taken from old horror flicks and their gruesome killing scenes. All text was hand written on front labels and the print finish is on a bulky uncoated stock to give the feeling of an old horror movie flyer.

JUNG VON MATT

Product: Wine Labels
Client: Gut Oggau

ATELIER TYPOUNDSO & THOMAS OTT

Product: Pizza Box
Client: Pizza Pronto
Material: Corrugated cardboard

Illustrations taken from the series "la grande famiglia"
by Thomas Ott.

PiZZA PRONTO

- Pizza Alaska
- Pizza Al Capone
- Pizza Arrabbiata
- Pizza Buffalo Bill
- Pizza Capricciosa
- Pizza Della Nonna
- Pizza Diavolo
- Pizza Funghi
- Pizza Gorgonzola
- Pizza Hawaii
- Pizza Mare Verde
- Pizza Margherita
- Pizza Marinara
- Pizza Melanzane
- Pizza Napoli
- Pizza Padrone
- Pizza Parma
- Pizza Pollo Pronto
- Pizza Prosciutto
- Pizza Prosciutto e Funghi
- Pizza Quattro Formaggi
- Pizza Quattro Stagioni
- Pizza Rucola
- Pizza Rustica
- Pizza Salame
- Pizza Siciliana
- Pizza Tonno
- Pizza Tonno Pronto
- Pizza UK Bacon
- Pizza Vegetariana
- Pizza Venezia

PIZZA PRONTO

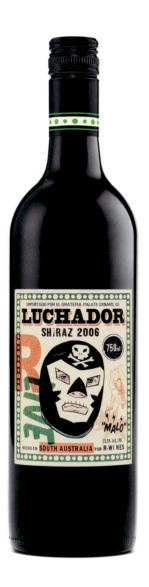 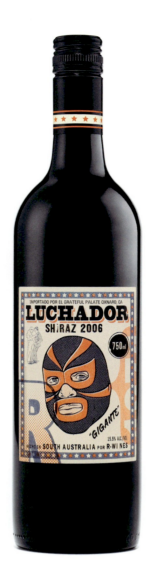 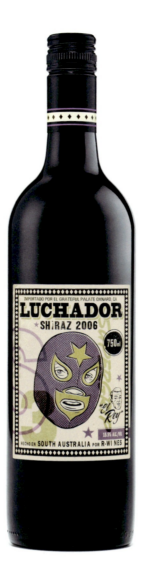 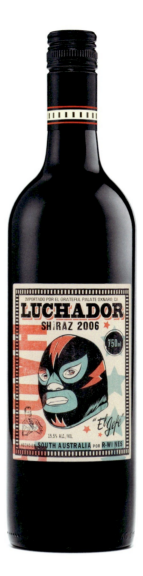

MORNING BREATH INC

Product: Luchador Shiraz
Client: The Grateful Palate / R Wines
Material: Glass bottles, paper labels, and corrugated cardboard

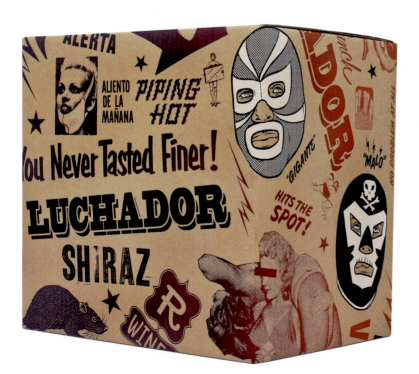

HOUSE INDUSTRIES

Product: Street Van Font Kit
Material: Offset-printed clay-coated kraft board

WE BUY YOUR KIDS

Product: Nelson Beer/Sneaky Rafter
Client: The Taboo Group/Nelson Beer

HOUSE INDUSTRIES

Product: House33 T-shirt Boxes
Material: Offset-printed kraft board

LAUREN GOLEMBIEWSKI

Product: Question Taste!
Material: Glass, paper, wood, corrugated cardboard

Question Taste! is a line of hot sauces inspired by the Dada movement. Each sauce is given a nonsensical name, Twing, Raskley, Zoost & Zingy to carry the Dada theme. The concept is that people must question conventional taste, and make it their own through this line of hot sauces, just as Dada questions aesthetics. Though, beware because the sauces come in four levels of intensities, yet give no indication of which sauces is hottest or mildest. The sauces come in an explosive little carrier so that the flavour adventure can be stored together.

NATHANIEL ECKSTROM

Product: Teaboxes
Client: Lala Land – Home and Human Fashion
Material: 355 gsm snowcard

Launched in April 2009 by Home and Human Fashion's label – 'Lala Land', the tea boxes are an innovative product that have not been created before. The four boxes each designed for special occasions – 'Happy Birthday', 'Happy Healthy Newborn', 'You're Wonderful' & 'Thank you' each combine visual art, typography and tea. Tea drinkers, non tea drinkers and tea appreciators will all be targeted as this product will offer a great gift idea due to the packaging. Good design reconnects us to our humanity by giving us excitement and pleasure. Lala Land tea is wonderful, beautiful and magical. It is a special gift that triggers emotions and wows peoples perception.

STINA PERSSON

Product: Spot-Less Blemish Gel
Client: Face Boutique
Material: Aluminium 8 ml tube and cardboard
outer carton

Product: Sweep Clean Cleanser on a Cloth
Client: Face Boutique
Material: Recyclable PE

Product: Fresh Faced Moisturiser
Client: Face Boutique
Material: Aluminium 60 ml tube and cardboard
outer carton

Product: Hair Laundry Shampoo
Client: Face Boutique
Material: Recyclable PE

REMO CAMINADA

Product: Andreas Caminada
Fine Food Products
Client: Andreas Caminada &
Globus Switzerland
Material: Cardboard 450 gsm

HARTUNGKEMP

Product: Vanilla Carmels Uptown Snacker/
Chocolate Cookies/Easter-Chocolate
Bunnies & Chicks/
Chocolate-covered Marshmellows/
Orange Carmel Pop/Licorice Twists
Client: Route 29

Gourmet confections company Route 29
tapped HartungKemp to update their branding
and create consumer packaging that would get
their treats noticed in the competitive candy
marketplace. We developed a bold and fun
new look that unified the historic brand – from
package structure to product naming to package illustrations. "Our caramels and chocolates
have never looked so tasty," said Route 29
owner Kim Kalan.

SKINNY SHIPS

Product: Jell-o
Client: Jell-o
Material: Cardboard

By introducing a cast of fun stylised characters
and a visual vocabulary that feels fresh and
fun, the new Jell-o identity burst with vibrancy
and joy.

JESSE KIRSCH

Product: Gubble Bum
Client: Gubble Bum

A fun and twisted approach to packaging for a line of flavoured bubble gum. The characters are comprised of nothing more than full and half circles; yet despite this extreme simplicity, their faces still manage to convey a wide range of emotions. Beneath the cutesy exterior, however, lies an unexpected twist: removing the outer box reveals the skeleton of each „bum."

MATS OTTDAL

Product: Drinking Yogurt
Client: Frisk

HELVETICA INC

Product: Spalab Shea Butter & Honey
Client: Kanebo home products

Product: Spalab Yogurt & Kiwi
Client: Kanebo home products

THE ROBIN SHEPHERD GROUP

Product: Brew Bottles & Taps
Client: Bold City Brewery
Material: Glass bottle, wood

The Robin Shepherd Group helped build Bold City Brewery's brand from the ground up, creating a main logo for the Jacksonville brewery, in addition to separate logos for each ale. The Robin Shepherd Group built illustrations that incorporate the Jacksonville skyline and the unique quirks of the brewery and the city. Subjects include Duke, the resident brew hound, an injured and vengeful manatee from the nearby St. Johns River, and "Killer Whale", the Brew Master's childhood nickname. As the brand continues to grow, each logo maintains the levity, hospitality, and hometown pride that Bold City Brewery is now known for.

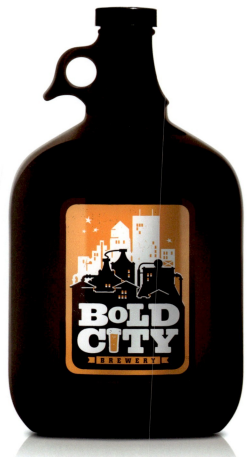

PEARLFISHER

Product: Innocent Smoothies
Client: Innocent

BVD

Product: Candyking
Client: Candyking International Ltd.

TURNSTYLE

Product: Baby Fuel Packaging
Client: Full Tank

Full Tank Baby Fuel is the first frozen baby food to combine the benefits of home prepared veggies with the convenience of portability. Baby Fuel packages the freshest organic ingredients in a travel-ready easy open squeeze pouch that fits in your pocket or purse and can even be eaten without a spoon. Full Tank Secret Agent Pastas "hide" organic veggies in the sauce so kids won't know they're eating them.

PEARLFISHER

Product: Dr Stuarts Teas
Client: Dr Stuarts

Graphic design, identity and creative insight.

JANINE REWELL

Product: Spork Packaging
Client: Personal project / RISD
Material: Cardboard

TDA ADVERTISING & DESIGN

Product: Shrewd Foods
Client: Shrewd Foods

Logo & packaging for all-natural brownies.

LAUREN GOLEMBIEWSKI

Product: Dirt Bath
Material: Plastic, paper

Dirt Bath is a line of bath & body products for young boys. The concept solves the problem of young boys' unwillingness to bathe. They would rather be playing in the dirt, so why not let them get clean while doing so? The products entice boys to have good hygiene while having fun. A dirt monster adorns each product to show boys how to scrub with dirt. The actual products are all natural and are made to look like mud.

HATTOMONKEY

Product: Milk Cocktail
Client: By Joe
Material: Carton

Hattomonkey has created a packaging design for the milk cocktail "By Joe". It looks like a well-known hero. It is easy to create Batman's ears. Hattomonkey designers have created a brand new package form. It looks familiar and is well-known since childhood.

EUGENE AND LOUISE BAKERY

Product: Chocolate Bar
Client: Eugene and Louise Bakery

ANDRÉ GIACOMUCCI

Product: Packaging Urussai
Client: Urussai
Material: Kraft paper

The packaging has two parts that fit together and close a box. After removing the T-shirt you can use it as a box or you can open it and the two parts became a character (that will change with the collections).

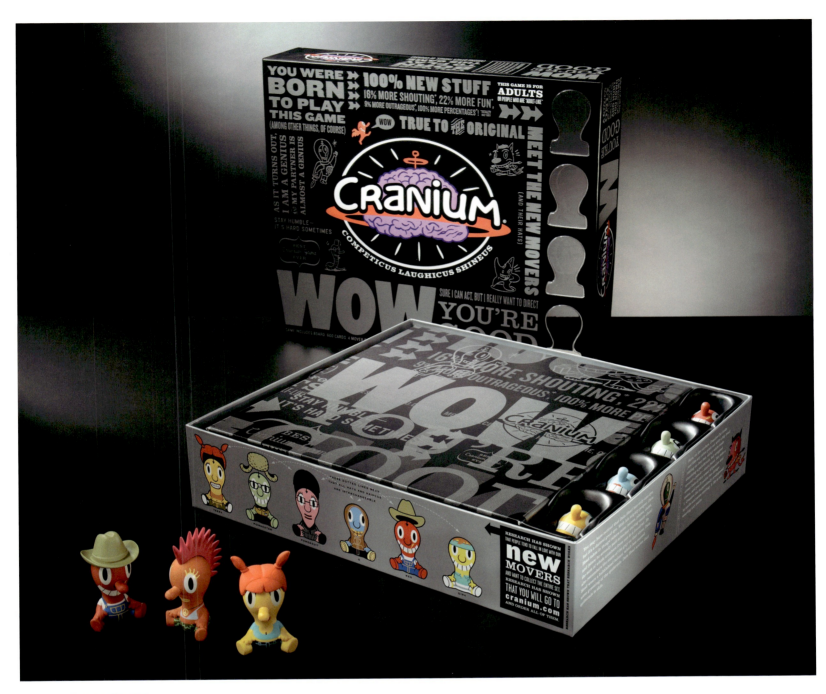

SANDSTROM PARTNERS

Product: Cranium Wow

MAX ZUBER

Product: Packaging for chocolates
Client: Péclard Zurich
Material: Carton, paper covering

High quality carton box with 5-colour print on paper covering. Various typical Zurich decors by famous Zurich painter Max Zuber.

NATE WILLIAMS

Product: Olive Uni-Sex Poop Bags
Client: Olive
Material: 65% post consumer kraft paper
and metal lid

Canister packaging for 100%
biodegradable dog poop bags.

HATCH DESIGN

Product: Wine Packaging
Client: Michael Austin Winery

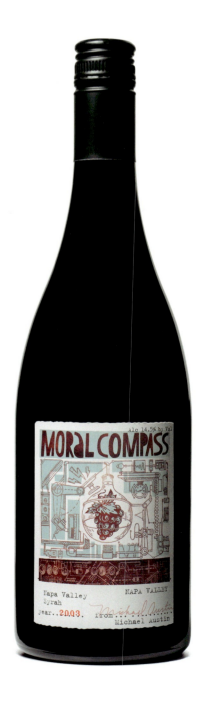

MASH

Product: Mollydooker Wines
Client: Mollydooker
Material: Fasson Estate 8
[Label paper stock]

Reinforcing the brand identity: The aims
were to create packaging that in no way
reflected that of any of their competitors,
that stood out from the crowd and that communicated the hands-on approach that the
wine-makers take in producing their wines.
The labels were created entirely from hand-
drawn illustrations, even down to the use
of the hand-drawn typeface. Not a single
font in sight. Inspiration came from antique
book patterns and 1930s advertising and
cartoon illustrations.

MITRE AGENCY

Product: Drink and Custard Cups
Client: Kernel Kustard
Material: Coated paper cups, printed

Product: Sandwich Box
Client: Kernel Kustard
Material: Coated paper box, printed

PEARLFISHER

Product: Jme Homeware
Client: Jme

TURNSTYLE

Product: Sausage Packaging
Client: CasCioppo Sausage

ROYALT

Product: Cigars & Tobacco
Client: Debonair Cigars & Tobacco

ANDY MANGOLD

Product: Monopoly Repackaged
Client: Personal
Material: Mat board, wrapped in inkjet
printed cream Arches Cover

The final package is just over 10" x 10" x 1.5" and includes
smaller containers for all of the various pieces and cards and a
laser-cut holder for all of the houses and hotels.

YVONNE NIEWERTH

Product: Pudding/Tyten
Client: Design Study

EDUARDO DEL FRAILE

Product: Tapas
Client: Tapas Wine Collection
Material: Paper label

MOUSEGRAPHICS

Product: Masticha Greek Product
Client: Saradis S.A.
Material: Plastic

STUDIO RAŠIC

Product: Self-promotion
Client: Studio Rašic
Material: Paper label

MITRE AGENCY

Product: Coffee Bean Bags
Client: Brew Nerds Coffee

Silver plastic lined coffee bags with white closure sticker printed, displaying different nerdy coffee images.

LOUISE FILI LTD

Product: Matches
Client: Mermaid Inn

This was a low-budget but effective way to produce matches.

PETER GREGSON STUDIO

Product: The Manual Co. Boxes
Client: The Manual Co.
Material: Cardboard, paper

Packaging design for hand made leather accessories.

IRVING

Product: Antipasti
Client: Carluccio's
Material: Clear self-adhesive labels

Inspired by handwritten price tickets in Italian food markets, Irving hand wrote simple labels and printed them on clear self-adhesive labels to allow the food to 'speak' for iteslf.

R DESIGN

Product: WH Smith Artist Materials
Client: WH Smith
Material: Glass, paper, plastic, card, aluminium

BIG FISH

Product: Belvoir Cordial Bottle
Client: Belvoir Fruit Farms

PETER GREGSON STUDIO

Product: Wanted Snacks
Client: Aroma Food

Visual identity for new nut packaging (pistachios, cashew nuts and peanuts).

BLEND-IT

Product: Mediterranean Restaurant
Client: MEZE

PETER GREGSON STUDIO

Product: Sopocani 100% Juice
Client: Monastery Sopocani
Material: Glass, paper

Brand, packaging and visual identity for
home made juices and delectable products.

IRVING

Product: Delicatezze
Client: Waitrose Ltd.
Material: Cartons

Irving created simple and appealing
designs inspired by Mediterranean
ceramics.

NOSIGNER

Product: Kanypo Udon
Client: The Oyama chamber of commerce and industry
Material: Vinyl, paper

PETER GREGSON STUDIO

Product: Woman Paper Bag
Client: Hairstyle Studio – Woman
Material: Paper, cotton

FELIX LOBELIUS

Product: Kaffe
Client: Kaffe
Material: Uncoated paper

Kaffe is a coffee shop started by four Swedes, thus the name ('kaffe' is coffee in Swedish). The handwritten charcoal aesthetic derives from the personal connection every person has with their type of coffee. This is reflected in a direct style of communication, with business cards, bags, take away cups etc. personally addressing the customer.

BIG FISH DESIGN LTD

Product: Tea Packaging
Client: Clipper Teas ltd.

GRAFIKART

Product: La Mariposa Wine
Client: La Mariposa/Viñedos De Alcohuaz
Material: Glass, ink, aluminium alloy

Digital offset on paper complex aluminium alloy.

BUG AGENCY

Product: Vin De Pays Label Wine Range
Client: Carrefour

EDITH LEVIN

Product: Sedies Sunflower Seeds
Material: Paperboard

I went with earth tone colours and a tree trunk texture on the boxes, while adding colours that relate back to the flavour of the seeds. Illustrations of the flavours, the logo and all the typography were done by hand, giving it all a truly organic feel. The seeds come in a large pack, as well as a smaller sample size – for those that just need a little taste before committing to the bigger size.

IMAGEHAUS

Product: Poly Seed Bags
Client: All Seasons Wild Bird Store
Material: Poly Bags

The objective was to create unique packaging for the Wild Bird Store's private label bird seed, which was unique but followed the new look and feel we had created. Bird lovers needed to be drawn in by the design and then purchase for the quality.

INSITE

Product: Wine Bottle Labels
Client: Five Rows Craft Wine
Material: 5 colour litho on uncoated pressure sensitive label stock

To convey the sincerity and authenticity of small batch winemaking, we created a label by hand – illustrating the logotype and painting the art on the side. As well, the packages are hand numbered and produced in small numbers to avoid waste while striving to make an intense and meaningful connection with the customer.

MASH

Product: Velvet Glove Wine
Client: Mollydooker
Material: Velvet flocking paper stock, metallic silver foil & French saver bottle

The top wine in the Mollydooker range. The 'Velvet Glove' wine uses a hand drawn design on a velvet flocking paper stock with a metallic silver foil. A wax dipped top on an French Saver bottle completes the package. The hand drawn design includes a diecut glove shape and handwritten text.

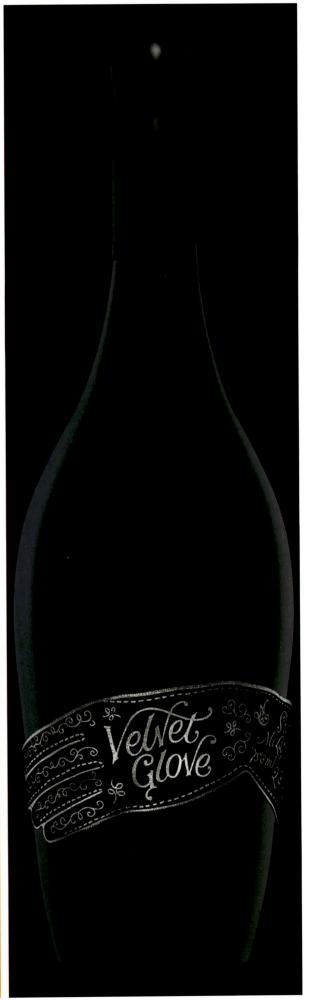

ELMWOOD UK

Product: ASDA Californian Wines
Client: ASDA

**TURNER DUCKWORTH:
LONDON & SAN FRANCISCO**

Product: Le Tourment Vert Absinthe Francaise 2008
Client: Distillery Vinet EGE

ID BRANDING / LILY CHOW

Product: Absinthe/Trillium
Client: Integrity Spirits

**TURNER DUCKWORTH:
LONDON & SAN FRANCISCO**

Product: Root: 1
Client: Click Wine Group

MORUBA

Product: Castillo de Maetierra Wines
Client: Vintae

KOEWEIDEN POSTMA

Product: House Wines
Client: Hema

DESIGNKONTORET SILVER

Product: Packaging Design ICA Yoghurt
Client: ICA AB

CATALINA ESTRADA URIBE

Product: Bossa Nova Super Fruit Juices
Client: Bossa Nova Super Fruit Company

MUCCA DESIGN CORP.

Product: The Gracious Gourmet
Client: The Gracious Gourmet

The clean, minimal typography and bright colour palette of the packaging lend a modern, sophisticated appeal, while classic botanical illustrations communicate the all-natural, homemade essence of the products.

AARON HINCHION & JOE HOLT / ALBION

Product: Lily's Kitchen: Proper Pet Food
Client: Lily's Kitchen
Material: Compostable recycled paper, water based inks

We wanted it to feel modern but have a timelessness to it. Something that says: "The food in this tin is quality" without resorting to pictures of the food or the usual big dog face. It has a nice wood cut quality to it. We then coloured each flavour, using certain colours to stand for certain foods, developed a logo and some organic icons.

CONCRETE

Product: Sula Lip Balm
Client: Sula
Material: Card stock

Sula is a new perfume/cosmetics line from Susanne Lang Parfumerie. Targeted at a younger audience than the company's senior brand, Sula allows customers to express their personal character and style by playfully layering different fragrances. Concrete developed the brand identity and packaging for various scents and cosmetics products. The line is distributed internationally through leading retailers.

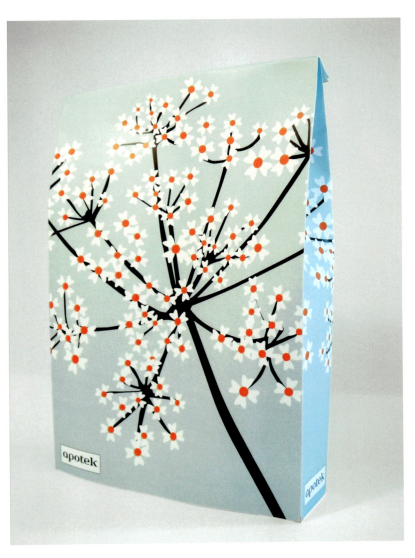

THORBJØRN ANKERSTJERNE

Product: Paper Bag
Client: Apotek
Material: 250 gsm coated paper

MOXIE SOZO

Product: Fruit and nut bar packaging
Client: Probar

CATALINA ESTRADA URIBE

Product: Tin Box
Client: Levi's

BRAVELAND DESIGN

Product: MOD Wine Label
Client: The Grateful Palate
Material: Adhesive coated label with gloss ink highlights

The wine label resembles the most recognisable object of the MOD movement; the scooter. The wrap around label features an attention to detail that is an important aesthetic to the music, fashion movement. The blue scooter label is for the white wine label and the red scooter label is for the red wine. Red and Blue are classic colours of the MOD movement that originated from the target icon.

Product: MOD Wine Cartons
Client: The Grateful Palate
Material: Cardboard paper

Each carton is colour coordinated for a white and red wine. The graphics wrap around the four sides and top flaps to create a complete visual experience for MOD that relates to the wrap around wine label on the matching bottles.

ANNA GESLEV, YOTAM BEZALEL

Product: Igloo – Ice Cream Parlour Chain
Client: Igloo Ltd.

The changing colours of the elements and the fact that the graphic language has many elements express the value of individualism, empower the experience in the stores, provide a fresh feeling of sweetness and fun and project an innovative concept.

HELLO MONDAY

Product: Sandwich On Wheels
Client: Drive By Sandwich

Product: Wrapping a Deli
Client: Yellow Deli
Material: Recycled paper

JEFTON SUNGKAR

Product: Fiesta Party Snack
Client: The Relish
Material: Card

ANNA DABROWSKI

Product: Sweet 2009
Client: Concept/Prototype

FROM CONTAINER TO CONTENT
REUSE, REUSE, REUSE

IN THE PAST, packaging was waste waiting to happen, surface instead of substance. What remained after opening the box was a byproduct with no practical function – wrapping paper and unknotted bows scattered across the living room floor, reminding us of the anticipation lost in the very act of opening our gifts. Today this situation is being very occasionally remedied by the creation of wrappers that become as valuable as the product that is protected and promoted within – the elevation of packaging from container to content.

Consumers' concerns about packaging usually centre on ease of use and ease of storage, greater convenience and less waste – function, not aesthetics. No doubt for equally pragmatic reasons, typography and copy-driven packaging have also come into focus recently, championed by consumers who are willing to spend more time on, and put more thought into, their purchases. But the recent practical approaches to packaging design take functionality to a whole new level, transmuting packing materials into products in their own right.

By generating an alternate function for the cast-offs, designers give each a second life as something that may last even longer that the product it once guarded. The Y Water bottle for a children's beverage by Yves Béhar of San Francisco's fuseproject, a jack-shaped plastic bottle filled with a candy-coloured liquid that is reusable as a building-block toy, like large-scale Lego, if the kids collect (and drink) them. German designer Anna Dabrowski's Cleanse water bottle doubles as a carafe. The raucously tilted recyclable PET vessel holds approximately eight glasses of water and can be resealed via a foil closure.

Folding is a mechanism crucial to some of the cleverest hybrid packing-products: The Hanger Pak by Steve Haslip arrives in a corset-shaped raw cardboard packet, but when opened can be cut apart and folded into a clothes hanger. Anni Nykänen's Pop-Up Popcorn Bowl concept for Packlab at Finland's Lahti Institute of Design takes folding further. Like a Chinese fortune-telling game, the kernels are sold in a flat, square package that folds open into triangular "petals" to become a four-legged bowl after the popped corn is removed from the microwave.

The multiple personalities of these packaging designs encourage an appreciation of banal objects, and add not just value but surprise to the experience of our everyday belongings. Progress Packaging in the UK champions the use of some oil-based materials such as nonwoven polypropylene, according to founder Simon Farrow, for this very reason. "We promote the reusability of the material rather than the recycled argument," he explains. "We genuinely believe that reusable items are the answer where possible, because even many recycling processes generate a huge carbon footprint, which must be taken into account as well."

ANNA DABROWSKI

Product: Sweet 2009
Client: Concept/Prototype

antipodes

SPARKLING

To be at your table today this water has been brought to the surface from the deepest water aquifer in New Zealand It has spent decades under enormous pressure in vast underground canyons more than 200 metres below the surface This pressure from within the aquifer creates a natural filtration process that has led to antipodes being scientifically categorised as the deepest, highest quality artesian water in New Zealand It has then been bottled at source providing a purity, clarity and taste that can only be found deep down at the end of the earth. Gently carbonated with the finest bead, antipodes is the perfect partner for fine foods.

DRINK CHILLED. DRINK OFTEN. LIVE WELL.

1000ml

Antipodes Water Company, 121 Customs St West, Auckland
New Zealand Artesian Water www.antipodes.co.nz

ANTIPODES

Product: Table Water
Client: The Antipodes Water Company

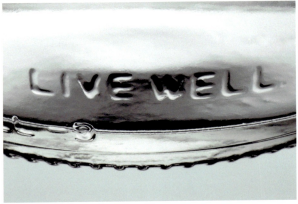

YVES BÉHAR / FUSEPROJECT

Product: Water Bottles
Client: Y Water
Material: Extrusion blow-moulded plastic bottle, injection-moulded plastic cap and die-cut recycled paper labels

The first 'Y'-shaped bottle is immediately recognizable, eliminating the need for additional labelling and more insipid branding methods (by locating all product information like bar codes and nutritional data on a biodegradable hangtag, fuseproject were able to keep the bottle itself bare. It is also re-usable, after the beverage is consumed, either as a tap water bottle or as a constructor set or Lego-type game, reincarnating the packing as a playful learning toy. The biodegradable natural rubber Y-Knot connects bottles together and provides a plethora of "building" possibilities. The design is in line with the company's goal to let kids be creative; its slogan "Y NOT" encourages kids to think on their own terms.

ICON DEVELOPMENT GROUP

Product: Tresdon Convertible Wine Packaging System

Tresdon is a wine packaging system developed with the manufacturer, retailer, consumer, and environment in mind. It carries and contains bottles of wine, but after purchase can be reassembled into a modular wine rack, thus encouraging recycling and reuse rather than disposability. Tresdon is made entirely of natural, biodegradable materials. It fits together by friction, without the use of adhesive materials.

KANELLA

Product: Sweet 2009
Client: Kanella
Material: Metal, white 120 gr. paper, black sealing wax

Kanella's boxed set of one dozen chocolates represents the twelve months of the year. Taken together, the bars function as a confectionary calendar. Wrapped in white paper, each is illustrated with an uncluttered image that evokes one month (February, for instance, features a Valentine's Day rose). The illustrations consist of charmingly retro-modern patterns that might have been spit out by an old dot-matrix printer and which match the design studio's corporate identity. At the back of each wrapper, Kanella notes the days of each month and provides delightfully random details about the illustration (February offers interested readers botanical information on the rose). Sealed with black wax imprinted with the studio monogram, the candy has been given (at least the air of) a rather sweet pedigree.

CUL DE SAC

Product: Olive Oil Bottle
Client: Mil del Poaig
Material: Wood, ceramic, mesh

Spanish designers CuldeSac designed the packaging for upstart olive oil brand, El Mil del Poaig. The half-litre bottle, containing oil made from thousand-year-old olive trees, is made of traditional Valencia ceramic (a marriage of bisque and glazed porcelain) and arrives cradled inside a wooden crate. The softly curved bottle was made to allow the consumer to savour every drop of the oil. The text was inspired by Roman history and based on manuscripts written during the same period in which the millinary trees were planted. Each bottle is covered by the traditional mesh in which the olives are harvested from the trees and then packed in a hand-made wooden crate that contrasts with the smooth alabaster refinement of the limited-edition vessel.

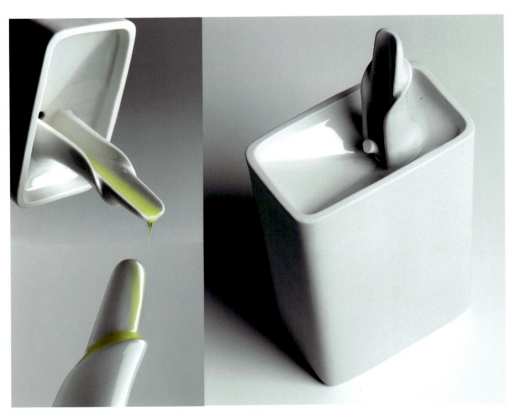

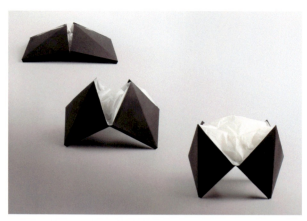

PACKLAB

Product: PopBowl

Folded like origami, this packet of popcorn kernels is sold and placed in the microwave flat, but as it heats, the popping corn "pops" up the packaging into a four-legged bowl for easy snacking.

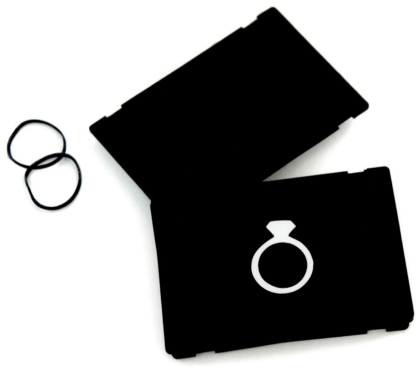

BYAMT INC

Product: Silver/Gold/Platinum Diamond Ring
Material: Lasercut and etched museum board, rubber bands

Remove the rubber bands from this cardboard container and open the box to find one of byAMT's Silver, Gold or Platinum Diamond Rings. The boxes come in either black or white and in three thicknesses in order to accommodate the 2mm, 4mm and 9mm rings. Each is constructed from lasercut layers of 1/16-inch black museum board that is laser-etched with graphics on the front and back. Inside, depending on the thickness of the ring it contains, a circular bed has been lasercut into the middle layers of board like a cushion that has been made-to-measure for the precious object it protects.

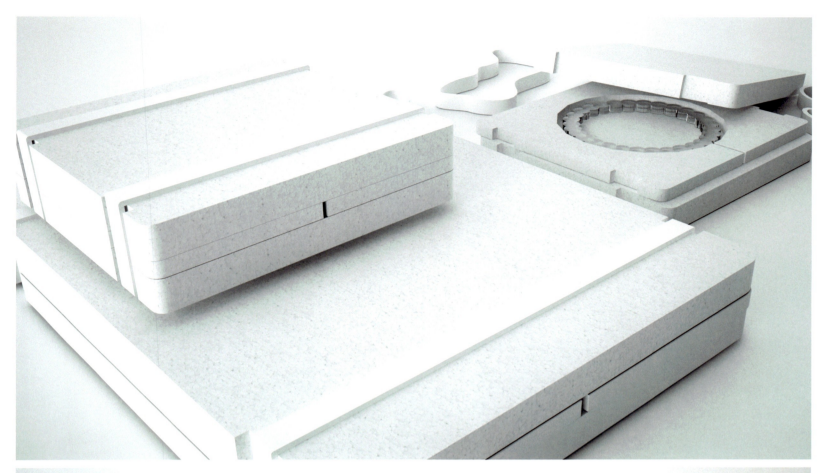

BYAMT INC

Product: EPS Acrylic Necklace Packaging Concept
Material: Expanded Polystyrene – EPS, rubber bands

Styrofoam packaging sandwiches the byAMT Acrylic Medal of Honor,
Ribbon of Honor or Juliana Necklaces and is secured by thick rubber
bands of matching colour that slot into notches cut on four sides.

PHIL WAREING

<u>Product:</u> Individual Pyramid Teabag
packaging
<u>Client:</u> 't' (private label)
<u>Material:</u> 300g MC silk and cardboard

This teabag packing uses no adhesives and,
after being cut, can be folded using just one
hand.

GABE RE

<u>Product:</u> Arcadia Tea Packaging
<u>Client:</u> Arcadia Organic Tea
<u>Material:</u> 100% recycled French muscle tone
paper, black non-toxic screen printing ink

This green design accompanied a naming and
branding project for an ecofriendly tea company. The triangular leaves of the individually
wrapped bags were created from a single
sheet of paper folded origami style in order
to keep production costs low. Each set of
four nest back-to-back in its packing.

MOXIE SOZO

<u>Product:</u> Shelter Box Packaging
<u>Client:</u> GoLite
<u>Material:</u> Corrugated cardboard

MEG GLEASON

Product: Biscuit!
Client: Student work
Material: Paper, cardboard

Using slotted coloured cardboard, this cracker packing is the product of the student designer's interest in Russian Constructivism. Users, after consuming their biscuits, can "deconstruct" or flatten their package, or take it apart in order to construct a second object. The package can be stacked and displayed in several ways to suit various retail environments.

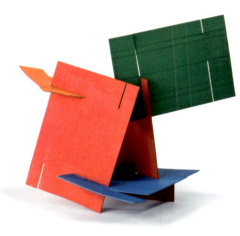

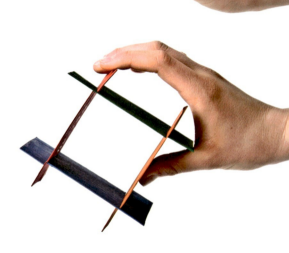

MEG GLEASON

Product: Chocolate Fest Packaging
Client: Student work
Material: Paper, cardboard

This cut and folded paper strawberry shelters a strawberry-flavoured truffle. The package was proposed by a student as a promotional item for a chocolate festival. The concept behind the festival identity was to focus on the moods, feelings and expressions of a person while they are savoring a piece of chocolate.

YIYING LU

Product: Magic Bean –
Let's Grow Together to Reap Great Rewards
Client: JWT
Material: Brown and corrugated paper

SHADES OF GREEN
TAKING RESPONSIBILITY

PERHAPS BECAUSE there are so many shades of sustainable "green", consumers have become the victims of "greenwashing", the trend to attribute ecofriendliness to earth-hostile products, processes and materials in order to make a greenback. Responsible packaging can take many forms: Sometimes it is recycled or recyclable, reduces waste or reduces the amount of material used in the first place. It cuts down or eliminates toxins from adhesives, bleach, inks and dyes. Simon Farrow of the UK's Progress Packaging, which has done catalogues for furniture manufacturer Established & Sons and boxes for the multidisciplinary design agency, Winkreative, uses sustainable inks and biodegradable materials that are now capable of matching the gloss and finish of older, more familiar, less sustainable methods. FSC-approved papers give his designers a broad range of choice in the creation of boxes, binders and printed pieces. For textile-based products – Progress has made tote bags for Art Basel Design Miami, Converse and Wallpaper – Farrow favours ethically sourced products like unbleached canvas. But there are a plethora of ways to go green, including extending the life of the package through reuse.

Responsible packaging may not even be sustainable per se, but it is nonetheless desirable so long as it protects and preserves responsible products like organic, local or fair trade food. In such a case, its design will increasingly reflect the all-natural, good-for-the-earth character of the contents through the use of unrefined packing materials, rustic typefaces, or the clear windows or glass that invoke the purity of the product within. It is worth noting that even responsible products – organic food, biological dishwashing liquid – in plastic bottles still produce waste. Sometimes, however, the use of plastic can redeem itself because it tends to reduce the amount of material consumed in the first place and diminish shipping weight – two important green goals. The moral of the story? Plastic, despite its bad-boy reputation, remains a lightweight, durable and therefore re-usable material.

There are, however, alternatives to the plastic bag (already outlawed in China, thank you very much). The now-ubiquitous "I Am Not A Plastic Bag" canvas tote forms a set with the (rather good reminder) "I Am a Plastic Bag And I Am 100% Recyclable" bag. But shopping bags are being developed from compostable materials today, as well. 60Bag.com bags biodegrade within 60 days after use and are as beautifully textural as chipboard. The inner linings of Magdalena Czarnecki's brown-paper bag-toys (This is a Monkey, This is a Bird and This is a Frog) are printed with the dotted-line pattern of origami animals that can be folded from the opened sack.

Designed by TDA, Newton sneakers come in a raw, unbleached paper-pulp box moulded into the shape of the shoes it contains in order to reduce the amount of material used.

Celery Design Collaborative calls packaging a "necessary evil" and works to make it part of the product experience. The studio's Lemnis Lighting asks how to persuade consumers that they will save money by spending $25 on a mercury-free, LED-based bulb (that will last 35 years). The solution? Design the packaging so that buying a Lemnis feels different from buying an ordinary incandescent. Celery wrapped the light in a circular sheet of recycled paper that folds into a tapering flat-topped box on the retail shelf. When opened, however, its perforated inner lining can be used as the lampshade. The package looks as innovative as the product is, adds value to the purchase and accommodates the brand's green ethos by being reusable.

"Our product is simple: water in a box," says Boxed Water Is Better founder and designer Benjamin Gott. "Our package is simple, a rectangular box. The product itself is the logo. Our product is our brand and our brand is our product." Gott wanted to take a mass-market item and lower its environmental impact while funnelling some of his profits into worthwhile projects like world water relief and reforestation. He used the reassuringly familiar box as the canvas and container for his product. While the technology behind cartons has changed quite a bit over the past 50 years, including being made from almost 90% paper, it is still a classic object. Gott printed "Boxed Water Is Better" on the boxes in an obscure variation of Helvetica. "This reflects our brand's appreciation of simplicity but it also stands out beautifully on the shelf in the sea of blue-tinted and overdesigned bottled water brands," Gott explains. Plastic bottles have an indefinite shelf-life, which in a nuclear war might prove helpful, but is problematic environmentally. Cartons don't last as long – they have a"shelf-life"–which is precisely the point that Gott is trying to make.

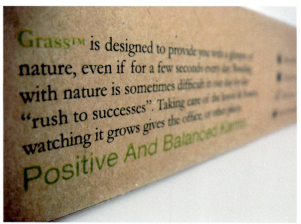

NINE99 DESIGN

Product: Grass Squares
Client: Student project/Shenkar College
of Engineering and Design, Israel
Material: Recycled paper

Grass tiles invite Mother Nature into the office or home. Inspired by Frank Lloyd Wright's Fallingwater and the architect's attempt to combine the artifice of building with nature, the product and packaging are made from recycled materials. The paper packages have an air opening to extend the shelf life of the product. The minimalistic design and logo are intended to let the living tiles breathe and give an organic aspect to the product.

YIYING LU

Product: Magic Bean—
Let's Grow Together to Reap Great Rewards
Client: JWT
Material: Brown and corrugated paper

Not quite as powerful as Jack's magic beans, this product is nonetheless a feat of biotechnology. Magic Bean consists of seeds laser-inscribed with letters and characters which, when they grow into plants, will bear the same inscription on their leaves. Using this technique, the designer etched the client's name in individual seeds and buried them in a planter box. When the client receives this raw corrugated cardboard package and follows the instructions within, they will be able to read the seemingly magic words after the seed has grown. In this way, JWT and Yiying Lu tell their clients that they look forward to growing together in order to achieve results.

ADAM PATERSON

Product: GrowYourOwn
Material: 100% recycled corrugated cardboard

This packaging contains fruit and vegetable seeds for novice gardeners. Using user-centric research and the innate properties of 100% recyclable corrugated cardboard, the new wrapper is simple, clear, sustainable and as approachable as its contents.

BENJAMIN GOTT

Product: Water Cartons
Client: Boxed Water is Better

SWEAR WORDS

Product: Egg Cartons & Box
Client: Green Eggs

BVD

Product: ChariTea/ChariTea Green,
ChariTea Black and ChariTea Red/
Lemonaid
Client: LemonAid Beverages GmbH
Material: Glass bottles with direct print

These teas are packaged in a classic standard clear glass bottle that feels good in the hand and looks authentic and straightforward rather than over-designed, without becoming banal. The ChariTea brand and product information reads clearly and tranquilly against the background of each tea colour. Noisome labels are eliminated by printing the graphics directly onto the bottle.

SCOTT AMRON

Product: New Soap, Old Bottle
Client: Bottle & Sell/New Soap, Old Bottle
Material: Salvaged bottles

New Soap is an eco-initiative. Its goal is to make it as easy as possible for companies to package their products in repurposed bottles, giving the consumer a greener option. The company cleans, sanitizes and processes old bottles for reuse as packaging for liquid soap. Bottle & Sell is able to save two bottles (the one that would have been manufactured as well as the one rescued) for each bottle sold. Rescuing and repurposing existing packaging is as responsible as design gets, but parents should warn their little ones to not take a sip from the new bottles.

ANDERS WILHELMSON

Product: Biodegradable Bags
Client: Peepoople AB

The Peepoo project was initiated in 2005 by the architect Prof. Anders Wilhelmson as a response to the urban situation in the world's fast-growing informal settlements. A research team was formed with the Swedish universities KTH and SLU. The design concept and the self-sanitation technology was awarded a PTC World patent in 2008. The company Peepoople AB was formed in 2006 to develop, produce and distribute the Peepoo. The mission of Peepoople is that everyone who so desires shall have access to dignified and hygienic sanitation.

CELERY DESIGN

Product: Lemnis Lighting Packaging
Client: Lemnis Lighting
Material: Recycled paper

MAGDALENA CZARNECKI

Product: This is Origami
Client: World Wildlife Federation (Self-initiated student project)
Material: Craft paper, uncoated paper stock

Empty paper bags contain simple step-by-step instructions on how to fold each bag into an origami animal, in order to create your own sustainable designer toy. The cost of the bag is directed to the World Wildlife Federation to help save endangered animals.

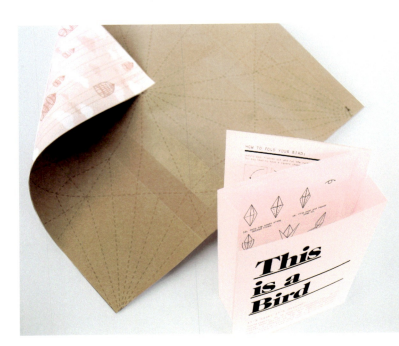

LENNIE DICARLO

Product: Salt Packaging
Client: xroads Philippine Sea Salts
Material: Box made of nipa palm, bow made of abaca, paper made of cogon grass, abaca and salago fibers

Unique to the Philippines. The handmade box is woven from nipa palm and the bow from abaca twine, a species of palm and banana native to the islands. The handmade paper attached to each box is from cogon grass, abaca and salago fibres. Our retail packaging is eco-friendly and 100% biodegradable. The nipa box provides the perfect vessel to hold your sea salt. Available in 5-oz size.

BLEND-IT

Product: Eco Dishes
Client: Annica
Material: Craft paper

A pair of Israeli entrepreneurs have joined forces with manufacturers from the East to develope a line of single-use, disposable utensils made from palm leaves and produced using energy-saving, low-cost methods. On the box, the integration of an illustration of a human figure communicates the brand approach to creating accessible, sustainable, quality products designed around the user.

ÉMILIE BERTRAND-VILLEMURE

Product: Electronics Packaging Concept
Client: Student work/University of Québec
at Montréal/Prof. Sylvain Allard
Material: Corrugated cardboard

Sick of the electronic retailers' blister-pack
approach to packaging? Bertrand-Villemure
suggests using good old corrugated board to
accomplish three things: Protect the environment, give a second life to a package that
consumers will want to keep and use, and
add allure to an ordinary product.

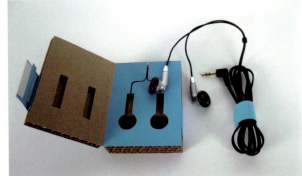

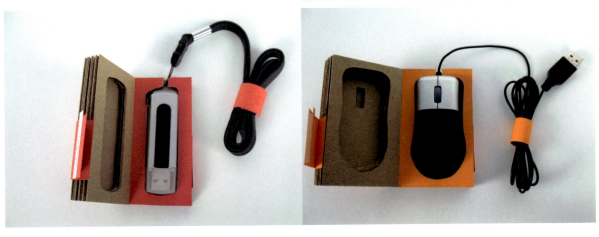

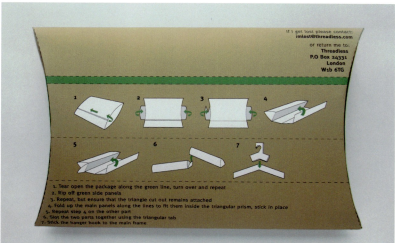

STEVE HASLIP

Product: Hangerpak
Client: Self-initiated
Material: Recycled card-
board

The pillow pack form is used for its strength, to ensure that its contents arrive in one piece. After recipients tear open the package, they may now fold it into a coat hanger on which to hang the T-shirt that came in the box. The packaging-cum-product could be made from recycled card or plastic, the only waste being the green tear-away tab – less than 5% of the material used.

VIIDRIO

Product: Flower-Tech 1.0 and Inner Labyrinth Shirt Design and Packaging
Client: VIIDRIO
Material: 100% cotton threads, aluminium tin, 100% recycled printed matter, aluminium foil tape

To link both items, shirt and packaging, the designers used embroidery. Both the illustration on the shirt and the embellishment to the package are embroidered in coloured thread. The packaging was created to be reused, if so desired.

TDA ADVERTISING & DESIGN

Product: Newton Running Shoe & Box
Client: Newton Running
Material: Moulded paper pulp

TDA created a moulded paper pulp box in
the shape of a pair of nested running shoes.
This reduces waste – and might just be easier
to jog home with.

ZAK KLAUCK

Product: Nike Shirt and Windbreaker
Cardboard Packaging
Client: Nike 100+08 Beijing, China
Material: Recycled cardboard

Product: Nike Shoe Packaging
Client: Nike 100+08 Beijing, China
Material: Recycled cardboard

The packaging for this shirt and windbreaker
was constructed from a mesh wrap cut
from recycled cardboard. The resulting bag
features a die-cut handle for easy carrying.
Because Nike produced them in a limited
edition, universal graphics were printed on
the packages and sizes were hand written on
the bag.

THORBJØRN ANKERSTJERNE

Product: Bio Bag
Client: Student project
Material: Paper

A statement to be carried around – and to carry other things around even if they have less to say.

STORMHAND

Product: Atelier LaDurance/
Promotional Japanese Denim Packaging
Client: Atelier LaDurance
Material: Bamboo wrap (44.5 cm x 26 cm) with velcro closure and black silkscreened text

Atelier LaDurance is a small, independent French denim label that emphasises the finest craftsmanship in its products. AL produces limited runs that are exclusively made of only the highest quality denim. The promotional Japanese Denim packaging is used as a site-specific medium developed for the retail environment. Its design demonstrates the refinement of Japanese craftsmanship in traditional selvage denim manufacturing.

Product: Atelier LaDurance/
Promotional Japanese Denim Packaging
Client: Atelier LaDurance
Material: Cheese cloth with silkscreen print

This polo packaging is re-usable. Crafted in an inexpensive loose-woven cotton known as cheesecloth that is typically used to strain and wrap pressed cheeses. Today it is available in seven grades, from open to extra-fine weave. The designers used the textile as an alternative to plastic shopping bags.

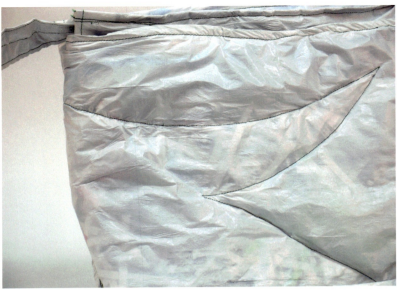

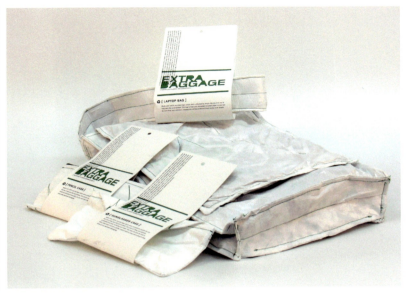

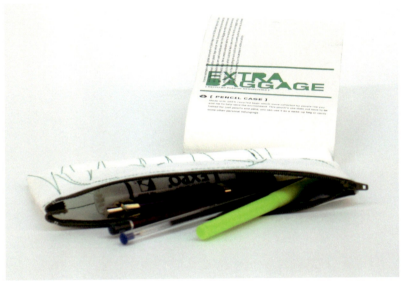

AMANDA MOCCI

Product: Extra Baggage Bags, Sleeves and Carrying Cases
Client: Student work / University of Québec at Montréal / Prof. Sylvain Allard
Material: Repurposed plastic shopping bags

Mocci collected basic plastic bags from local shops, generated her materials by heating the bags in layers with a pressing iron and then sewing them into bags, sleeves and cases with – appropriately – green thread.

60BAG

Product: Oval Bag
Client: 60BAG
Material: Non-woven flax-viscose

An alternative to polypropylene "green bags" and to the thick plastic bags offered by most retailers, 60BAG is a biodegradable carrier bag made from a patented non-woven fabric produced in Poland from the byproducts of flax fibre manufacturing. This process saves natural resources and minimizes energy use during the production process. Once a 60BAG is thrown away, it decomposes within 60 days, without the need for expensive recycling or disposal in landfill. The bags, which are available in various shapes and sizes, can be backyard composted or even burnt.

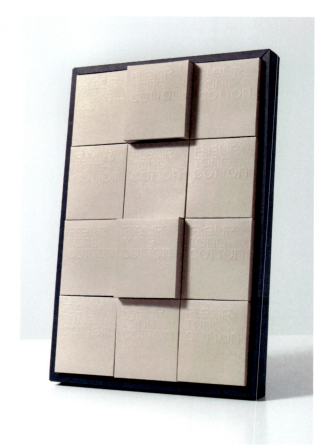

HOMEWORK

Product: Packaging
Client: Fleur Tang

KARIM CHARLEBOIS-ZARIFFA

Product: Sugar Packets
Client: Student work / University of Québec at Montréal / Prof. Sylvain Allard

Individual sugar stick packets made from corrugated cardboard, detachable
from the pack and sealed with caramel "glue" for sweet stirring.

AZUL AMUCHASTEGUI BARI

Product: Bird Perch & Packaging
Client: Student work / University of Québec at Montréal / Prof. Sylvain Allard

An ecological walnut perch and bird seed come wrapped with a simple belt
of paper and boxed with a bird-shaped window, respectively.

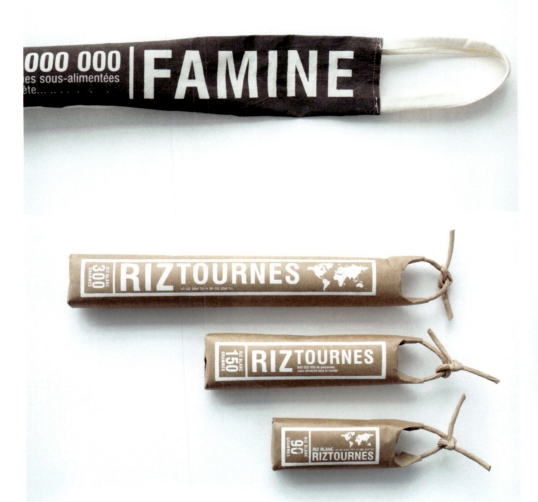

KARIM ZARIFFA

Product: Riztournes Bags
Material: Paper, fabric, rope

With these rice sacks, in three sizes plus a fabric bag for transport and refilling, Zariffa and Riztournes make a statement about world hunger. The small bags are printed with information about starvation around the globe while the tall bag is illustrated with a leg bone to recall an undernourished human figure.

MODULARITY
BUILDING
AN
EXPERIENCE

CONSTRUCTED PACKAGING involves the accretion of patterns, geometry, layers and forms, and adds value to the product beyond its material or function. This type of wrapper may include modular designs or folding techniques in either two or three dimensions: Australia's Mor bath and beauty products are packaged in real wood dispensers, but it's the company's cardboard constructions that are most striking. A box for the Dala product line layers silver, scarlet, faux woodgrain and mauve spheres to create a sophisticated, nearly sartorial texture. Albers Winery's Cabernet repeats a colourful Escher-like pattern in blues, reds, yellow and green on the box, the bottle's label and its foil seal. Hatmon's Cowmilk carton uses clusters of black, grey and red X's to draw a gentle bovine muzzle on its face. The carton is folded upward into two triangles at its crown to represent the cow's ears, a simple and charming version of constructed packaging.

Beyond its visual charm, however, packaging like this constructs an experience in the opening of the product. Packaging that becomes a spectacle, a tactile adventure – an aesthetic experience, a moment of play or Jack-in-the-box-like surprise, echoing the unwrapping of a longed-for gift – can enrich any purchase. Opening an Apple product is an experience with multiple rewards; the placement of objects goes beyond convenience to build anticipation, while boxes with magnetic openings or secret slots make the (expensive) purchase feel like a present – even the

Styrofoam is cut into an attractive filigree. Consumers have begun to post their "out-of-the-box" experiences with new gadgets online, so that this added-value experience has also become significant to the success of the brand. The greater the complexity of the constructions, the deeper the consumer's reaction to the discovery of the content within, which ultimately serves, and celebrates, the product, itself.

Today, folding and construction methods seem to be moving both forward and backward – for good reason, according to Simon Farrow of Progress Packaging. Advances in CAD sampling and prototyping give designers greater flexibility and encourage experimentation. "We have seen the influence of Oriental styles recently, where intricate folding and finishing combine to create simple lines and sharp edges on packs," says Farrow. "Conversely, the movement toward simplicity is seeing many packs going back to traditional methods of scoring and folding such as rhemus bending because these processes give an almost handmade, just-for-you finish." Made-to-measure design jumps from fashion into the shopping bag. Take it home.

MUOTOHIOMO

Product: SIS. Deli+Café Identity, Packaging & Interior
Client: SIS. Deli+Café

Muotohiomo's identity for a chain of Finnish delicatessens specializing in high quality ecological and organic products included the creation of the name, the identity and shop interiors, in addition to the packaging. Designers Rasmuss Snabb, Noa Bembibre, Aki Suvanto and Aleksi Perälä's goal was to create a strong identity for the franchise that would be simultaneously recognizable and flexible enough to give each store a unique feel. The packing reflected the earth- and human-friendly ethos of the brand in simple block lettering, brown paper sacks and a simple but unusual black-and-white plaid pattern on cups and take-out bags.

ALVIN CHAN

Product: Frame Shoulder Bag
Client: Frame Publishers
Material: Canvas

THORBJØRN ANKERSTJERNE

Product: Paper Bag
Client: Apotek
Material: 250 gsm coated paper

THORBJØRN ANKERSTJERNE

Product: Paper Bag
Client: Apotek
Material: 250 gsm coated paper

MEETA PANESAR

Product: Forbidden: Exotic Cocktails
Client: Self-initiated

This cocktail, containing alcohol, is designed to entice shoppers with symbols from the culture of ancient Arabia and its forbidden fruits, foods like the apple, pomegranate, or mint that were once believed to lure lovers into a naughty fantasy of lust and romance.

LINDSEY FAYE SHERMAN

Product: Houndstooth Peanut Butter for Dogs
Client: Houndstooth

MEETA PANESAR

Product: Op Art Wine – Merlot
Client: Self-initiated

Product: Op Art Wine – Shiraz
Client: Self-initiated

MEETA PANESAR

Product: Op Art Wine – Cabernet Sauvignon
Client: Self-initiated

The packaging for this wine was inspired by the colour schemes and designs of Joseph Albers and the Op Art movement.

INARIA / PROGRESS PACKAGING LTD

Product: Spa Range Shopping Bags and Boxes
Client: One & Only Resorts
Material: Paper, custom ribbon handle, paper-lined box

This luxury packaging set was designed by Inaria for a resort's spa product range. Progress precision foil-blocked intricate two-colour patterns on each piece.

EDENSPIEKERMANN

Product: Luxury Chocolate Branding and Packaging
Client: TCHO Inc./Technology + CHOcolate
Material: Paper and box wrappers, foilstamp, lacquer

Sweets wrappers use the square as the flexible foundation of a modular branding system. Typography and a geometric logotype distinguish functional elements from decoration. The colour scheme ranges from dark brown to bright magenta, orange and yellow, reflecting the different flavours and modernist values of the brand.

DARK CHOCOLATE "CHOCOLATEY"
Ghana
70% Cacao
60g (2.12oz)

DARK CHOCOLATE "CITRUS"
Madagascar (Sambirano Valley)
67% Cacao
60g (2.12oz)

DARK CHOCOLATE "FRUITY"
Peru
68% Cacao
Fair Trade beans
60g (2.12oz)

DARK CHOCOLATE "NUTTY"
Peru
65% Cacao
Fair Trade beans
60g (2.12oz)

DARK CHOCOLATE "CITRUS"
Madagascar (Sambirano Valley)
67% Cacao
60g (2.12oz)

PENTAGRAM DESIGN LIMITED

Product: Saks Fifth Avenue Shopping Bags
Client: Saks Fifth Avenue
Material: Paper, cardboard

MOR COSMETICS

Product: Nordica Dåla – Body Oil Box
Client: MOR Cosmetics
Material: Cardboard, silver hot-foil stamping,
debossing and spot UV varnish

Product: Nordica Freïa – Body Oil Box
Client: MOR Cosmetics

A scanned wood graphic, 4 PMS colours, hot-foil stamping
in silver and debossing were employed to layer graphical elements in
colourful, garment-like box designs.

MOR COSMETICS

Product: NORDICA Freïa – Lip Balm Box
Client: MOR
Material: Card with special treatments (Silver Hot
Foil Stamping, Debossing and Spot UV Varnish)

MOR COSMETICS

Product: Nordica Dåla – Hand & Body Wash Pump
Client: MOR Cosmetics
Material: Bamboo

This bamboo dispenser, etched and hand-painted,
was designed with reuse and collection in mind.

Product: Nordica Freïa – Hand & Body Wash Pump

MOR COSMETICS

Product: Nordica Freïa – Soap Bar
Client: MOR Cosmetics

The vegetable soap that fits inside
the bamboo box below.

MOR COSMETICS

Product: Nordica Dåla – Lip Balm Box
Client: MOR Cosmetics
Material: Cardboard with silver hot-foil stamping,
debossing and spot-UV varnish

MOR COSMETICS

Product: Nordica Freïa – Soap Box
Client: MOR Cosmetics
Material: Bamboo

MOR COSMETICS

Product: Nordica Dåla – Soap Box
Client: MOR Cosmetics
Material: Bamboo

Pop patterns are created through the exuberant use of graphics, vintage wood block type, and original illustrations.

Product: Whales Salt and Pepper Shakers

EMIL KOZAK

Product: Les Ettes Logo and
Identity Redesign
Client: Les Ettes

NARANI KANNAN

Product: Gotta Moo Eco-Friendly
Milk Packaging
Material: Bagasse moulded pulp paper

Kannan's 4-litre carton consists of two 2-litre interlocking cartons, which can be unlocked when the shopper returns home via a vertical sliding mechanism. The 4-litre dual container allows the milk to stay fresh and also makes it easier for children and the elderly to carry and pour with ease.

DESIGNBOLAGET

Product: Chocolate Bar Wrappers
Client: Moshi Moshi Mind
Material: Foil, paper

Product: Tea Canisters
Client: Moshi Moshi Mind
Material: Metal

Product: Vitamin Supplements
Client: Moshi Moshi Mind
Material: Jars with lids

DESIGNERS UNITED

Product: Tea Canisters
Client: Tea Route
Material: 250g metal box, silkscreen printing

AIRSIDE

Product: Konditor & Cook Packaging
Client: Konditor & Cook
Material: Paper and card

Taking inspiration from the art of cake making, Airside designed K&C's new identity
based on the swirling action of mixing
ingredients together. The pattern is such
that it can be used in part or whole, as
needed, and provides a background for the
logo. Icing and cake decorating determined
the colour palette.

TRIDVAJEDAN

Product: Optimo and Strukto Packaging
Client: Cemex-Dalmacijacement
Material: Natron paper with protective layer

For cement company Cemex-Dalmacijacement, Tridvajedan created the Optimo and
Strukto logotypes via an intervention in
typography. The basic graphic element consists of two illustrations of building objects
that clearly communicate the purpose of the
product: a house for Optimo representing a
cement used primarily by small craftsmen,
and tunnel for Strukto representing a cement
used in more complex construction projects.

BASE DESIGN

Product: Haircare Line (Concept)
Client: Fred Segal Beauty

For this 18-product hair care line, a spin-off of the Fred Segal
department store, Base used the brand's red and blue swirled stripes
as a springboard for the development of a set of similar striped
patterns, one for each package. In this design, Base questions the
contemporary dictate that logomarks are the only way to identify
a brand today. With Zorbit, Base sourced matte white bottles, jars
and tubes, and printed the swooshing stripes in high gloss, creating
a juxtaposition between the two finishes. All product information,
including the logo and ingredients were placed on the back.

TURNER DUCKWORTH:
LONDON & SAN FRANCISCO

Product: Camera Film
Client: Superdrug Stores plc

KOEWEIDEN POSTMA

Product: Photography Product Line
Client: Hema
Material: Various

The designs show graphic fan forms, inspired by
the diaphragm of a camera. Various, overlapping
transparent colours were used to differentiate
the different products within this line.

BUDDYCREAT

Product: Build Your Own Kaleidoscope Kit
Client: Tate Museum Britain

TDA ADVERTISING & DESIGN

Product: Bliss Organic Ice Cream
Client: Bliss Organic

TORU ITO

Product: Design Tex
Client: Shiseido
Material: PP

MOXIE SOZO

Product: U Hydration Packaging
Client: NUUN

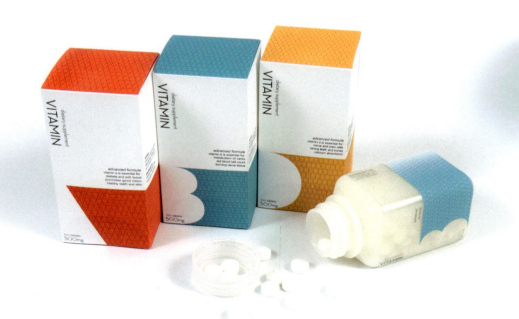

ROBERT FERRELL

Product: Silhouette Vitamins
Client: Student work
Material: Paper

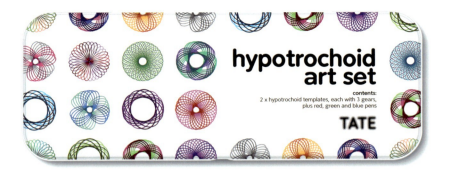

BUDDYCREAT

Product: Hypotrochoid Art Set
Client: Tate Museum Britain

BRAVELAND DESIGN

Product: SUXX Wine Carton
Client: The Grateful Palate
Material: Cardboard paper

This box and bottle label resembles the 1970s-era Lite Brite game with pixel graphics that enliven all surfaces of the carton.

BRAVELAND DESIGN

Product: SUXX Wine Label
Client: The Grateful Palate
Material: Adhesive coated label, gloss ink

CAMPBELL HAY

Product: Pastry Boxes
Client: Lola's
Material: Frovi board

These boxes emphasise the handcrafted nature of the cupcakes by using tactile materials and finishes. The brightly frosted cupcakes pop out as a surprise from the subtle exterior of the boxes.

ERWIN BAUER

Product: Weinquartier Wine
Client: Weinquartier

A repeating pepper pattern plays on the character of the wine. The typography, called Diseased Pen by Janto Lenherr was especially developed for the client.

ID BRANDING

Product: Lovejoy Vodka
Client: Integrity Spirits

Five bottles contain small-batch, handcrafted regular and hazelnut vodka distilled in Portland, Oregon. ID worked with the client to create a name that embodied both the spirit of Portland and of vodka, in general. ID selected the flask-like bottle shape and designed a series of four labels to be released simultaneously, allowing customers to choose the label that best suits their mood or the occasion.

HELVETICA INC

Product: Macaroon Sweetbox
Client: Hefti Jeuness

HATTOMONKEY

Product: Milk
Client: Milk Collection / Cowmilk
Material: Cardboard

Embroidery was once limited to fabric and was almost unheard of on paper. The cross-stitch package attracts attention for this very reason. A peculiar package construction creates cow ears at the top of the carton.

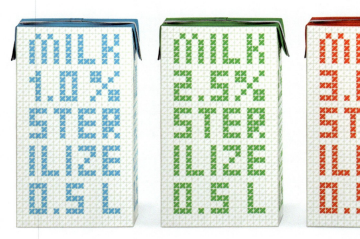

BASE DESIGN / MICHAEL YOUNG

Product: Passanha Olive Oil
Client: Herdeiros Passanha
Material: Glass

SCANTILY CLAD
THE VIRTUES
OF THE MINIMAL

MINIMAL PACKAGING communicates through understatement and clarity, no matter what the affordability or exclusivity of the market. Minimal labels feel subtle, true to their content and pared-down, if not stripped. Under Kenya Hara's direction, Japanese brand Muji has fashioned itself a paradigm of simplicity. The look and feel of its packaging is based, like its products, on the conviction that design should first communicate quality, function and value. Other minimal approaches make a virtue of the generic: The bare design of the Brand brand of plastic food storage products stands out from its overdesigned rivals by choosing to not stand out at all. "Resealable Sandwich Bags", the box reads. Nothing more, nothing less.

The Okotoyama Sake, Refined Sake and Ultra-Refined Sake bottles by British designer Jamie Conkleton articulate the sake-making process through the diminishing opacity of the three identically shaped bottles. To produce different grades of sake, proteins and oils are stripped from each rice grain so that the more the rice is polished, the finer the liquor produced; hence, Conkleton produced three bottles in opaque white, frosted and clear glass. Without the need to express quality grades, Passanha's Quinta da San Vicente olive oil bottles by Hong Kong-based Michael Young come in clear glass that allows the basic purity of the product to shine through the uncrowded block text printed directly on its surface. At the other extreme, Ode Oliva organic olive oil comes in a black jug; the name of the product serves as its only embellishment.

Minimalist packing often takes advantage of the legibility of classic typography, of which Helvetica is, perhaps, the reigning monarch. But minimal packaging doesn't waste its breath: text is limited to the essential. David Fung's milk cartons express the "staple" quality of milk by using bright planes of primary colours to outline the box – and very little verbiage.

As one might expect, the minimalist aesthetic is best applied to products that are their own best advertisements. Camille Lillieskjold's packaging for Habitat housewares (a towel, stacking racks, wine glasses) consists of simple neutral coloured paper strips that belt each product, leaving some, if not most, of the product exposed and allowing shoppers to both see and feel the item's texture and construction.

"Thought-driven design will always trump a pretty picture; the future of design is all about having a solid concept to build from," says Chris Zawada of Canada's Lovely Package. "Personally I find that our grocery stores aren't so much cluttered with boring designs as they are with over-designed scream-at-you-from-the-shelf designs. Packaging needs to have shelf appeal and presence, but it doesn't have to scream at the consumer."

Little Fury's common first aid items – travel-size doses of plasters and painkillers – come in naked cardboard packs embossed with the life-size outline of their contents. The front of the package describes those contents in plain English with the tagline: "Help. I've cut myself." Or "Help. I have a headache." Indeed, the dematerialization of the packing is the direction that savvy companies and thoughtful designers will go – and not out of the goodness of their hearts. "Companies will always find a way to reduce the amount of material they use," Zawada admits. "I'd like to think that it's to become more sustainable, but really it comes down to cost savings." Nothing more, nothing less.

BASE DESIGN / MICHAEL YOUNG

<u>Product:</u> Passanha Olive Oil
<u>Client:</u> Herdeiros Passanha
<u>Material:</u> Glass

BLOOM

<u>Product:</u> Johnnie Walker Black Label
<u>Client:</u> Johnnie Walker & Sons

KYM ABRAMS DESIGN (KAD)

<u>Product:</u> Beeline Honey
<u>Client:</u> North Lawndale Employment
Network
<u>Material:</u> 65 lb. bight white prekiss-cut label

A line of honey products developed to
provide training and jobs for Chicago's ex-
offenders.

LEWIS MOBERLY

<u>Product:</u> Waitose Mustards
<u>Client:</u> Waitrose Ltd.

WAREN DES TÄGLICHEN BEDARFS GBR

Product: Bier
Client: Waren des täglichen Bedarfs GbR

"Taste doesn't need a name," says the tagline. Enough said.

WESEMUA

Product: Extra Virgin Olive Oil/ Liquid Gold
Client: Aceites Únicos
Material: Metal

A canister designed to suggest that its content is comparable to liquid gold.

TURNER DUCKWORTH: LONDON & SAN FRANCISCO

Product: Honey Bee
Client: Waitrose Ltd

A simple typographic design, playing with the "E" in HONEY to form the striped body of a bee, but which also references wooden honey twizzler sticks.

ERIC HOFFMAN

Product: Honey Jars
Client: Bee Raw Honey
Material: Scientific grade glass, aluminium lid

ESPLUGA+ASSOCIATES

Product: Vives Gau Wine
Client: Bodegas Vives Gau

Four years ago, Vives decided to limit his wine production to 9,000 bottles in favour of extremely high quality organic production. On the pack, the designers featured a simple large "V" to represent the owner's commitment to superior quality. The "V" in Vives also represents the word "verdad", meaning truth in Spanish.

MORUBA

Product: Arar Wine
Client: Arar
Material: Silkscreen and label

Because they were packaging a wine that turns Rioja on its head, the designers upended the typographical character "A," making the letter a representative element for the label and the brand. Beside being the initial of the trademark and surname of the winery's founders, it represents the leading-edge style of this new viticulture project.

FARMGATE

Product: Suncare
Client: Blockhead

The inspiration for these unique black and metallic silver sunscreen containers came from mobile phones, a must-have for Blockhead's target consumer. The all-important UV protection rating numbers were then made "brand-ownable" with the addition of a simple hash icon.

STOCKHOLM DESIGN LAB

Product: Notebook
Client: Askul

STOCKHOLM DESIGN LAB

Product: Notebook
Client: Askul

KYLE POFF

Product: North American
Cabernet Sauvignon
Client: Abacuser
Material: Glass, screenprinted ink

MORUBA

Product: Numbernine Wine
Client: Winery Arts

The graphical and conceptual solution for the Winery Arts collection revolves around the number 9, considered by many cultures to be a symbol of knowledge. Each wine from the Winery Arts collection has a particular symbolism that summarises the Numbernine concept.

ESPLUGA+ASSOCIATES

Product: Mesoestetic Men
Client: Mesoestetic

Packaging for a men's beauty product line that uses numbers to create a direct and simple but robust graphic line. Dark backgrounds with white text reach out in a strong, straightforward way to men.

JESSE KIRSCH

Product: Deep Water
Client: Deep Water

Clean typography along with a forthright caddy design makes Deep Water stand out on the bottled water shelves. Large white letters and a small droplet in pale blue allow the clear water inside the bottle to remain prominent. The caddy, with a self-holding joint, needs only a small sticker on the opposite end to remain closed. The sticker also serves as the product label including a barcode, price and other information. Two small notches in the caddy allow the customer to hold the 4-pack comfortably.

NOSIGNER

Product: Spirit of Japan Soy Sauce
Client: FUJITORA (prototype)
Material: Glass

The moment that soy source is at its most appealing is when it is poured into a small white dish in front of fresh raw fish. Nosigner's package captures this moment on a clean white bottle.

BVD

Product: Café Concept, Packaging Design, Stories
Client: Turesgruppen AB

Black, white and stainless steel meets warm wood, and evokes the old fashioned café in order to project quality, style and a modern, urban atmosphere. The graphics are clear, strong and simple, as well as surprising and playful: bits of stories are written on everything from porcelain to little packets of sugar.

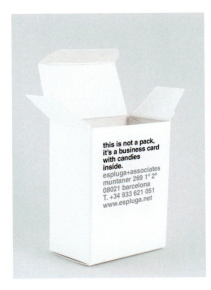

ESPLUGA+ASSOCIATES

Product: This Is Not a Pack
Promotional Box
Client: Espluga+associates

A self-promotional box that explores the
boundary between packaging and branding –
if any such boundary exists.

JAMIE CONKLETON

Product: Otokoyama Sake
Client: Self-initiated
Material: Glass

To create different grades of sake, rice
grain is polished to remove proteins and
oils. The more the rice is polished the better
the outcome. This process of refinement is
highlighted through the decreasing opacity
of each bottle.

CAMILLA LILLIESKÖLD

Product: Elements
Client: Habitat
Material: One-colour screenprint on card

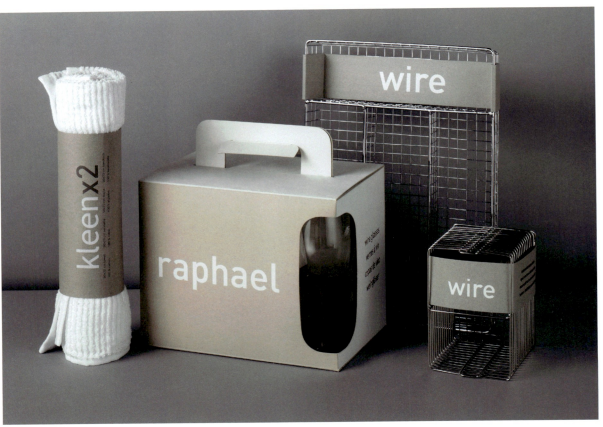

MICHAEL YOUNG

Product: Whisky Bottle (concept)
Client: Nikka Whisky
Material: Glass

MADE THOUGHT

Product: Chocolate Packaging
Client: Yauatcha

AVIGAIL BAHAT

Product: Canned Foods
Client: Platon
Material: Aluminium cans, pargament paper

Project at Graphic Communication
Department in Shenkar School of Design
and Engineering.

A series of packages for fruits, vegetables
and fish on which the food type is indicated
by colour and cans are bound in a triangular
acrylic pack. The label quotes Plato: "God
is the truth, and the light is its shadow" and,
in line with the philosopher's theories of
the "platonic" nature of things, the logo is
rendered slightly differently on each can.

MICHAEL YOUNG

<u>Product:</u> Whisky Bottle (concept)
<u>Client:</u> Nikka Whisky
<u>Material:</u> Glass

CONCRETE

<u>Product:</u> Perricone MD Cosmeceuticals
<u>Client:</u> Perricone MD
<u>Material:</u> Card stock

Following an unsuccessful packaging redesign that resulted in sagging sales and a loss of brand identity, Perricone MD commissioned Concrete to update the packaging design, among other things. Concrete developed a modern interpretation of traditional apothecary, using understated, elegant typography, scientific photography and frosted amber glass.

ALICE CHOCOLATE

Product: Chocolate Wrappers
Client: Alice Chocolate

A luxury Swiss chocolate produced in a glacial valley overlooking the Alps outside the chocolate-history capital of Bern that is intended to become "the definitive, 21st-century, all-artisanal, made-in-Switzerland, epicurean chocolate experience." The Alice sliding case is faced with an old-fashioned silhouette of a girl's profile, giving the box a heritage feel while its clean design also feels modern.

STORMHAND

Product: Chocolate Packaging
Client: Australian Homemade
Material: Greyboard, aluminium wrap

Greyboard, which is made from waste paper, is strong, flexible and cheap. The designer selected this basic material to create AH's premium packaging. A matt lamination prevents the inside of the box from becoming smudged when filled with chocolates and gives the exterior of the pack an unusual imperfect, tactile finish. A wide variety of motifs, representing different flavours, was printed with carotene on square chocolates so that the gem-like sweets establish a strong contrast between content and packaging. A sealed heavyweight aluminium wrap that spells 'absolutely pure' also reinforces this contrast.

RUIZ+COMPANY

Product: Chocolat Factory Bars
Client: Chocolat Factory

Following the brand identity's graphic style, which is "austere luxury," this new line of candy bars is defined by a colour scheme that corresponds to the type of cocoa used for each. The text provides only the most relevant information, such as the type of cocoa or where it comes from.

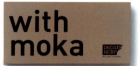

CIDCOM

Product: Mitzi Blue Chocolate
Client: Zotter / Mitzi Blue
Material: Alterna 300g, environmental-friendly paper

STUDIOKANNA

Product: Gift Box
Client: 4th floor

JESSE KIRSCH

Product: Tazaa Soap
Client: Tazaa Soap

Strong typography and a sharp colour palette define this packaging system for a line of six scented soaps. The bright white of the sleeve evokes cleanliness, while the interior box echoes the colour of the ingredients used in the soap. The initials of each scent's name are die-cut on the sleeve, revealing the colour of the box below. An opening at either end invites shoppers to smell the soap without opening the product.

NIMROD GAVISH

Product: Gooday – Organic Energy Supplements
Client: Visual Communication Department /
Shenkar College of Engineering and Design
Material: Metal, enhanced paper

LITTLE FURY

Product: Help Remedies – OTC Medication
Client: Help Remedies
Material: Co-moulded paper pulp,
corn-based plastic

Help Remedies is a line of Over The Counter
(OTC) medication aimed at making health
issues simple. The line's six products are
designed to guide the consumer through
confusing pharmacy aisles. The pack is
clean and minimal with user-friendly colour
coding and approachable cues that identify
the symptom clearly. It is also green, having
been manufactured using an innovative
combination of paper pulp and co-moulded
corn-based plastic so that it is compostible
and a first of its kind.

DAVID FUNG ONLINE

Product: Milk Redesign
Client: Self-initiated (concept)

YAIR GOLAN

Product: OD Dairy Products
Client: Self-initiated (concept)
Material: Plastic

The conceptual brand name OD is the Hebrew word for More. OD dairy products are an experimental project that puts the craving for fat at the centre of the product design. The packaging is meant "to attract consumers and make them want to grab it and eat it, right there and then," says Golan.

TOMORROW PARTNERS

Product: Vaska Detergents
Client: Vaska
Material: HDPE Plastic

Transparent materials, bold typography and strong lines set this package apart from from its shrill overdesigned competitors. The use of the circular handle is unique in the category and the bottle uses recyclable materials and earth-friendly production processes.

SORTDESIGN

Product: Luxury Chocolate Bar Range
Client: Co Couture
Material: Conqueror recycled laid, fresh white 300g

This folded textured card box has a spot-colour printed exterior and interior and foil blocked type on the front of the pack.

ESPLUGA & ASSOCIATES

Product: Hand Soap
Client: Chic & Basic
Material: a combination of Pet, aluminum, paper

Product: Barcelona Guide
Client: Chic & Basic

Product: Shower Gel
Client: Chic & Basic
Material: Transparent PVC

TDA ADVERTISING & DESIGN

Product: MIX1 Vitamin Drink
Client: MIX1
Material: High-density polyethylene

RUIZ+COMPANY

Product: Pack of Trousers
Client: Cooked in Barcelona
Material: Plastic containers
(mimicking take-away food tubs)

RUIZ+COMPANY

Product: Turrón Christmas Candy
Client: Chocolat Factory

RUIZ+COMPANY

Product: The Pasta Chocolate Products
Client: Chocolat Factory

MERRY MILK CHOCOLATE & HAZELNUT

MERRY CHOCOLATE & COOKIES

MERRY CHOCOLATE & ALMONDS

MERRY DARK CHOCOLATE & HAZELNUT

JESSE KIRSCH

Product: Truffle box, Shopping Bag,
Chocolate Bars and Tins
Client: Melt

GROOVISIONS

Product: 100%ChocolateCafe
Client: Meiji Seika Kaisha, Ltd.

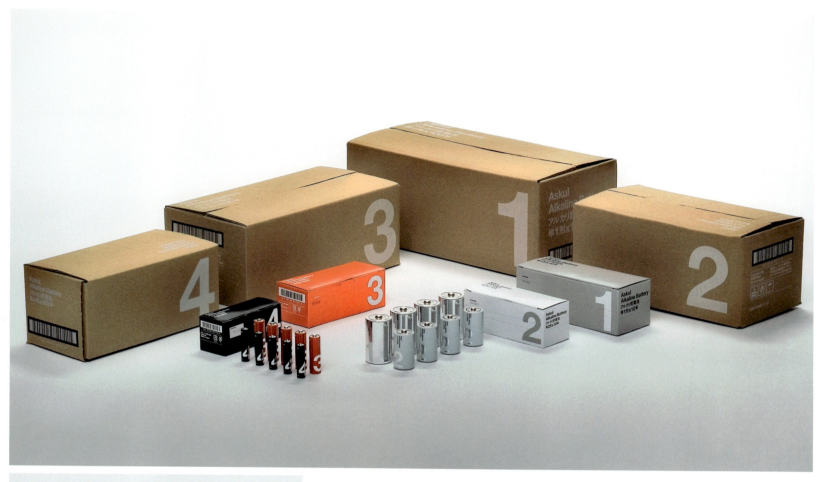

STOCKHOLM DESIGN LAB / SDL

<u>Product</u>: Batteries
<u>Client</u>: Askul

<u>Product</u>: Tape
<u>Client</u>: Askul

BRICAULT DESIGN

<u>Product</u>: Tea Series Chocolate Bars
and Percentage Series Chocolate Bars
<u>Client</u>: Thomas Haas Chocolate
<u>Material</u>: Cardstock

Bricault designed a chocolate bar mould
that creates unique pieces and turns sharing
into a game.

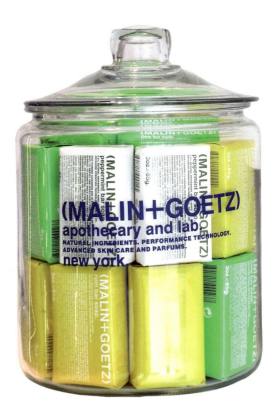

2X4

Product: Lime Bar Soap, Peppermint Bar
Soap, Rum Bar Soap and Large Soap Jar
Client: Malin+Goetz
Material: Paper, glass

STOCKHOLM DESIGN LAB / SDL

Product: Copypaper
Client: Askul

DOWLING DESIGN & ART DIRECTION

Product: John Lewis American White Oak Bathroom Accessories
Client: John Lewis Partnership
Material: UV-spot varnished cardboard

Dowling emulated the texture and colour of the oak wood product by replicating its grain on the box in a raised finish. Line illustrations of products are punctuated by white elements that pop.

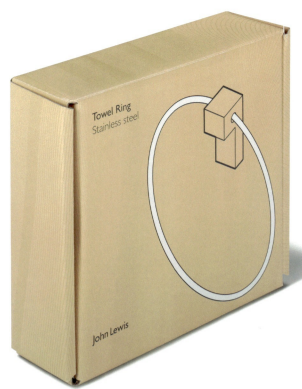

ESPLUGA+ASSOCIATES

Product: Phytomed Line
Client: Exiko Laboratories

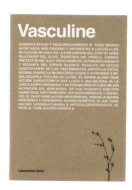

PEPE GIMENO

Product: Sivaris Rice
Client: NM Arrosos de Qualitat
Material: Recycled carton and paper

PEARLFISHER

Product: Store-Brand Frozen Meals
Client: Waitrose

DESIGNERS UNITED

Product: Diathlasis Bag
Client: Diathlasis Architectural Lighting
Material: Craft paper 110gsm, silkscreen
printing

JESSE KIRSCH

Product: Brand Food Storage
Client: Brand

A no-nonsense approach defines this line of
generic store-brand packaging. Helvetica,
greyscale colour palette, and newsprint-like
stock place these products in stark contrast
to the rainbow of loudly designed competitors lining supermarket shelves. The Brand
brand stands out from the masses by not
standing out at all.

ESPLUGA+ASSOCIATES

Product: Photogen System
Client: Mesoestetic

Packaging for beauty treatment products dealing with the photogen system,
the pack reflects the technological
improvement that this machine represents: a combination of technologies
and diversity of treatments. Each type
of treatment is easily identified by different colour tone and intensity.

STOCKHOLM DESIGN LAB / SDL

Product: Card Case
Client: Askul

Product: Ink Jet Paper
Client: Askul

BVD

Product: Pens
Client: Askul

STOCKHOLM DESIGN LAB / SDL

Product: Holder
Client: Askul

Product: Liquid Glue
Client: Askul

SID LEE

Product: Basic Nutrients and Beauty Dose
Client: Functionalab
Material: High-density polyethylene

The visual identity of Functionalab is the sum of three fields: science, nutrition and cosmetics. Text on the labels refers to the periodic table, invoking the spirit of the laboratory.

SÉBASTIEN MARTINEAU

Product: 66°
Client: Student work / University of Québec at Montréal / Prof. Sylvain Allard

SID LEE

Product: Tonic Range
Client: Functionalab
Material: Phial

SID LEE

Product: Personalised Pack
Client: Functionalab
Material: Cardboard

EDUARDO DEL FRAILE

Product: Soso Salts
Client: SosoFactory
Material: Plastic

ESPLUGA+ASSOCIATES

Product: Cosmedics by Mesoestetic
Client: Mesoestetic

The basic line of Mesoestetic looks basic, albeit refined in order to attract both beauty industry professionals and aesthetic doctors and individuals.

SHAW JELVEH DESIGN

Product: Mercury Paint
Client: Mercury Paint

BVD

Product: Electrolux Vacuum Cleaner/ Ultrasilencer Special Edition Pia Wallén
Client: Electrolux Floor Care and Light Appliances

A highly graphic profile distinguishes this vacuum cleaner, its retail hangtags and promotional material. The natural cardboard package features a glossy white interior, as if the box had been turned inside-out, and resembles the product itself. Included is a tote bag in recycled and new polyester that can be used later as a laundry bag. A typographical identity was screenprinted on the vacuums and looks industrial in contrast to the blank perfection of the product.

Stainless steel
large pruner
Solid ash
handles

John Lewis

Stainless steel
flower snip
Solid ash
handles

John Lewis

Gardening scissors

John Lewis

Bunting

John Lewis

DOWLING DESIGN & ART DIRECTION

Product: John Lewis Gardening & Outdoor Living
Client: John Lewis Partnership
Material: Grey boxboard, spot colour, reversed-out type

For an extensive range of John Lewis own-brand gardening and
outdoor living accessories, Dowling created a deceptively simple and
cost-effective packing solution that works across the entire range. A
spot colour with reversed-out type was printed on both sides of grey
box board, allowing the natural colour and texture of the board to
show through the type.

SHAW JELVEH DESIGN

Product: Cambridge Mesh Identity and Packaging
Client: Cambridge Mesh

BVD

Product: Fitness Product / Shapy
Client: Naturapoteket

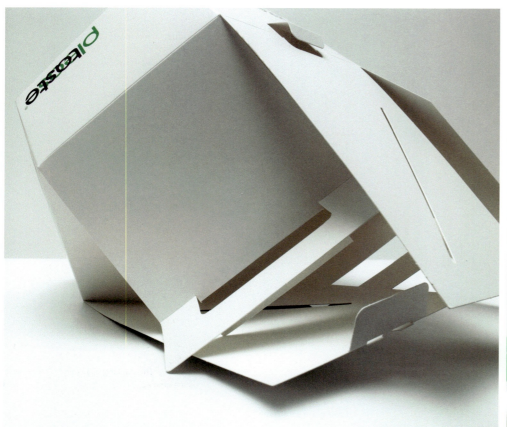

HOMEWORK

Product: Packaging
Client: TastePlease

GOODMORNING TECHNOLOGY

Product: Packaging for Digital Hearing Aid
Client: Widex
Material: Black, transparent folio, matt-coded cardboard, hard compressed foam, leather, double-moulded silicone

The hearing aid has become less clinical and more attractive today. Its packaging should be just as appealing. For Widex, boxes and pouches had to be suited to universal shipping for a multitude of hearing devices, its inner layers were designed to be modified by doctors to fit the appropriate content.

A transportation pouch inside provides maximum protection to the devices during shipping and yet maintains delicate touch points with the product. To achieve this, a double-moulded silicone container in the pouch is capable of cushioning the whole range. As the box and pouch are opened, a simple two-layer raster effect shows a sound wave spelling out the Widex slogan 'High-Definition Hearing'.

This is a matchbox made by Baxter of California in the United States of America.

We call it: "Firestarter".

It contains roughly thirty black wooden matches with white tips. You can use these matches to light our "Flammable" soy-based candle, ignite your Sunday bbq or burn whatever the fuck crosses your sick mind...

Baxter OF CALIFORNIA

This is a "Flammable" scented candle made by Baxter of California in the United States of America.

We call it: "Jasmin Noir".

It weighs nine ounces, that is two hundred and fifty five grams, and lasts for roughly seventy hours. It is made of a soy-based wax, hand-poured in New York by our friends at Joya.

MARC ATLAN

Product: Flammable Matches
Client: Baxter of California
Material: Offset on paper

Matches included as a gift in the flammable candle.

Product: Flammable Candle
Client: Baxter of California
Material: Foil and blind emboss on uncoated stock, silkscreened glass

The candle container is an old-fashioned and expensive single malt lowball tumbler: a masculine, familiar form. Graphic dots, echoing the glass dimples on the bottom, are silk-screened all over the glass using a subtle black-on-black pattern that is exposed as the candle burns down. A textural gridded dot pattern is also embossed around the box. Atlan used only one font, in only one size. "It became a bit of an obsession," he admits, "undressing the packaging to the max." The designer wrote a solid (sometimes deliberately irrelevant) text in an underdesigned running block of black foiled "body copy"-like lettering. The packing is as minimal then as it is maximized.

PENTAGRAM DESIGN LIMITED

Product: "Art in Transit" Tote Bag
Client: Cass Art London

DESIGNERS UNITED

Product: Promotional Packaging for the Film Festival Is
Client: Thessaloniki International Film Festival
Material: Metal box, silkscreen printing

PENTAGRAM DESIGN LIMITED

Product: Packaging Line Up for Heal's Department Store
Client: Heal's

ASYLUM

Product: Chocolate Packaging
Client: Chocolate Research Facility

Product: Blossa Annual Edition Glögg
Client: Pernod Ricard Nordic

This bottle that is shorter and rounder than other Blossa products. The company retains the broad outlines of their bottle from year to year, changing only the colours and typography to reflect a particular year's product design and flavour.

TURNSTYLE

Product: DRY Soda Bottle
Client: DRY Soda

In a fashion similar to fine wines, these sodas were developed specifically to be paired with foods. For this reason, DRY wanted the bottle to look at home in an upscale white tablecloth restaurant or a five-star hotel. Monochromatic, typographic and screen-printed labels boil product information down to their essence without extraneous flourishes. Minimal graphics on clear bottles puts the purity of the product on show. The owner's signature on each bottle denotes a sense of craft behind each soda recipe.

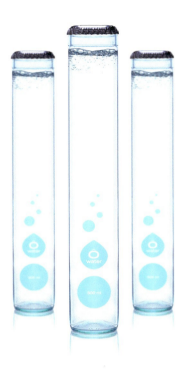

FERRO-CONCRETE

<u>Product:</u> Range of First Blush Juices
<u>Client:</u> Ferroconcrete – Branding Co./
First Blush, Inc – Client

AXYGENE

<u>Product:</u> Ô Water
<u>Client:</u> Axygene
<u>Material:</u> Glass tubed bottle
and twist cap

MOUSE GRAPHICS

<u>Product:</u> Iliada Olive Oil
<u>Client:</u> Agrovim
<u>Material:</u> Aluminium tin

STOCKHOLM DESIGN LAB / SDL

<u>Product:</u> Lingonberry Lemonade, Elderberry Lemonade
<u>Client:</u> Ikea Food

MALMBERG ORIGINAL

<u>Product:</u> Malmberg Original Beverage
<u>Client:</u> Malmberg Original

ERWIN BAUER

Product: Türk Wine
Client: Wine-Growing Estate Türk

MILLER CREATIVE

Product: Shirah Wine 2005 Harvest
Client: Shirah Wines
Material: Glass, cork, letterpress label, wax

ERWIN BAUER

Product: Wien Museum Wine
Client: Wien Museum

SWEAR WORDS

Product: McIvor Wine
Client: McIvor Estate
Material: Paper, silver foil, high build gloss varnish on logotype

NINE99 DESIGN

Product: Trixey Wine
Client: Student work

LEWIS MOBERLY

Product: Señorío de Arinzano identity
Client: Bodegas Chivite / Arinzano

RUIZ+COMPANY

Product: Lo Mon Wine
Client: Trossos del Priorat

NINE99 DESIGN

Product: Shefa–Young Wine
Client: Student work

SORTDESIGN

Product: Herb Packaging
Client: Love Olive
Material: Incada Silk 300g

Product: Organic Olive Jar
Client: Love Olive
Material: Paper label stock

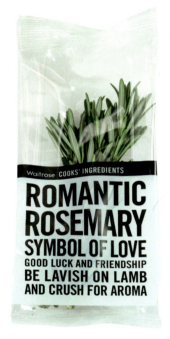

LEWIS MOBERLY

Product: Waitrose Cooks' Ingredients Fresh Herbs
Client: Waitrose Ltd.

STILETTO NYC

Product: The People's Pickle,
Mean Beans
Client: Rick's Picks
Material: Paper / satin polylaminate

LINDSEY FAYE SHERMAN

Product: Sweet Potato Chippers
Client: Want A Cookie Co. TM
Material: Label on plastic pouch

CONCRETE

Product: Xoco Chocolate Box
Client: Xoco

CONCRETE

Product: Xoco Chocolate Bags and Labels
Client: Xoco

HAMPUS JAGELAND

Product: Alton Brown Ingredients Range
Client: Alton Brown
Material: PLA plastic and recycled paper

PURPOSE

Product: Credit Crunch Chocolates
Client: Laura Santini

LEWIS MOBERLY

Product: Waitrose Cooks' Ingredients
Client: Waitrose Ltd.

PROGRESS PACKAGING LTD

Product: Established & Sons Tote Bag
Client: Established & Sons
Material: Unbleached canvas

PROGRESS PACKAGING LTD

Product: Design Miami Basel Bags
Client: Design Miami
Material: Nonwoven polypropylene

Pantone-matched nonwoven fabric was screenprinted and fitted with a diagonal stitched feature pocket on the exterior to give a layered effect.

MUCCA

Client: Brooklyn Fare
Material: Almost all 100% recycled paper

DESIGNERS UNITED

Product: The Languages of Tea
Client: Tea Route
Material: Craft paper 110 gsm / duotone silkscreen printing

DU wrote the word tea in various typefaces and in the languages of the origin countries of all Tea Route products.

THINK SIMPLE ACT SIMPLE

Product: Paper Bag
Client: Basheer Graphic Books
Material: 300 gsm matte art card

Printing on five surfaces disguises this paper bag as a giant and strongly graphical book.

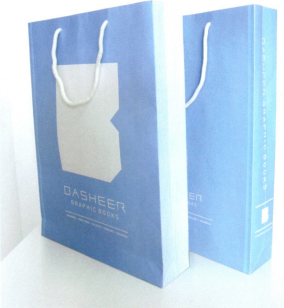

PENTAGRAM DESIGN LIMITED

Product: Art in Transit Tote Bag
Client: Cass Art London

PENTAGRAM DESIGN LIMITED

Product: Packaging Line Up for
Heal's Department Store
Client: Heal's

ASYLUM

Product: Chocolate Research Facility Bags
Client: Chocolate Research Facility

STOCKHOLM DESIGN LAB

Product: Swedish Sparkling Birch Sap
Client: SAV

ESPLUGA+ASSOCIATES

Product: Clos Galena Wine
Client: Clos Galena

GRAFIKART

Product: Montsecano Pinot Noir
Client: Montsecano
Material: Glass, ink, aluminium alloy

DESIGNERS JOURNEY

Product: Falling Feather Wine
Client: Arcus As

BLEND-IT

Product: Boutique Winery
Client: Adir Winery

LEWIS MOBERLY

Product: Warre's Warrior Reserve Wine
Client: Symington Family Estates /
Warre's Warrior

EDUARDO DEL FRAILE

Product: O de Oliva Olive Oil
Client: The Natural Oil Company
Material: Glass, paint

By designing the jug to resemble a pharmaceutical product, Fraile suggests that the product is beneficial for the health. The opaque bottle preserves the quality of the oil.

DESIGNERS JOURNEY

Product: Siglo de Oro Wine
Client: Arcus As
Material: Clear-on-clear label and paper

The letters DE in a bold gold foil are combined with the Chilenean coat of arms to underline the origin of the wine. A secondary label towards the base of the label resembles currency communicating exclusivity and premium quality.

R DESIGN

Product: Selfridges & Co. Grocery Range
Client: Selfridges & Co.
Material: Glass, paper, plastic

LISA LLANES

Product: Fellas Grooming Products
Client: Fellas

LISA LLANES

Product: S+A Beer and Grilling Utensils
Client: Steak & Ale (s+a)

HATCH DESIGN

Product: Wine Bottles
Client: Maclean Winery

HELVETICA INC.

Product: Pasticcino Dolce Sweets
Client: Hotel Nikko Tokyo
Material: Dense fibreboard, fabric tag

Designed for a renowned boutique hotel in Tokyo, this series of packages comprises four elements: an outer cartonboard container and three cylindrical drums containing confectionary. Details have been kept to a minimum on the exterior. The finish is deliberately understated to create anticipation for the disclosure of the primary packaging within. Duotone photographic imagery and a small fabric tag provide the only ornament.

Product: Hartford Reserve
Client: A&P

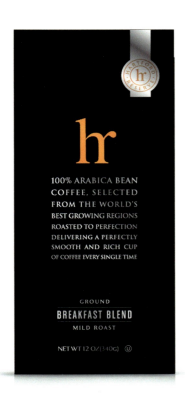

ERWIN BAUER

Product: Zull Wine
Client: Wine-Growing Estate Zull

LEWIS MOBERLY

Product: Selfridges House Labels
Client: Selfridges & Co.

INHOUSE DESIGN

Product: Dada 1 Wine
Client: Dada

THORBJØRN ANKERSTJERNE

Product: Adnams Beer
Client: Adnams
Material: Screenprint and labeling

HATTOMONKEY

Product: Drinking Water
Client: Niagara

DESIGNERS JOURNEY

Product: Lysholm Sodd Aquavit
Client: Arcus As

DESIGNERS JOURNEY

Product: Moel Wine
Client: Arcus As

DESIGNERS JOURNEY

Product: Santé Wine
Client: Arcus As

DESIGNERS JOURNEY

Product: Atlungstad Aquavit
Client: Arcus As

SKINNY SHIPS / RICHARD PEREZ

Product: 16 oz Bottle
Client: Stiegl

Retaining the brands extensive elements—bold blackletter logo treatment, the staircase icon, and deep crimson red—maintained familiarity within the brand. But updating and incorporating new elements, such as the diagonal rising label that mirrors the upward motion of the staircase logo, brings a contemporary feel to the traditional brew.

MUCCA

Product: Schiller's Liquor Bar
Client: Windy Gates SoHo / Keith McNally

The house wine at Schiller's is sold in three grades: cheap, decent, and good. Customers can choose from these three grades of wine and the actual varieties and vintages rotate on a regular basis. We created a labelling system that uses large white stencils to print the actual words "cheap," "decent," and "good" directly on the thick glass decanters. Since we worked closely with the architects and interior designers to create the overall experience of the restaurant we were able to help devise a rack system that was consistent with the brand.

ERIC HOFFMAN

Product: Acerola Logo and Wordmark
Client: Drill Inc. for Nichirei Foods
Material: Shrink-wrapped label on glass and / or plastic

ERWIN BAUER

Product: Lustig Wine Primeur
Client: Estate Lustig

A stylized pattern of silkscreened wine leaves in high gloss UV coating was created for the background of the opaque labelling rolls. The special Primeur wine series visualizes the sparkling character of the young wine by capturing the letters of the wine name in bubbles representing carbonation.

TDA ADVERTISING & DESIGN

Product: Honest Foods Granola
Client: Honest Foods

HELVETICA INC

Product: Reset Blend Tea
Client: Natural House

SILVER

Product: Food Packaging and Identity
Client: Renée Voltaire AB

BIG FISH

Product: Breakfast Cereal Box
Client: Dorset Cereals

BRICAULT DESIGN

Product: Hot Chocolate Mix
Client: Thomas Haas Chocolate
Material: Steel, paper

An oval can maximizes the surface area of the canister face and, once the product is used up, the label can be peeled off to reveal an attractive, reusable can with subtle branding.

TURNSTYLE

Product: Chai Packaging
Client: Jaipur Avenue

LANDOR ASSOCIATES SYDNEY

Product: Coffee Packagings
Client: Good Company Coffee
Material: Foil bag

Product: Pleasure Experts Bags
Client: Chocolat Factory

This shopping bag is one of a three-part series, each with a different message about pleasure, which is the focus of the campaign.

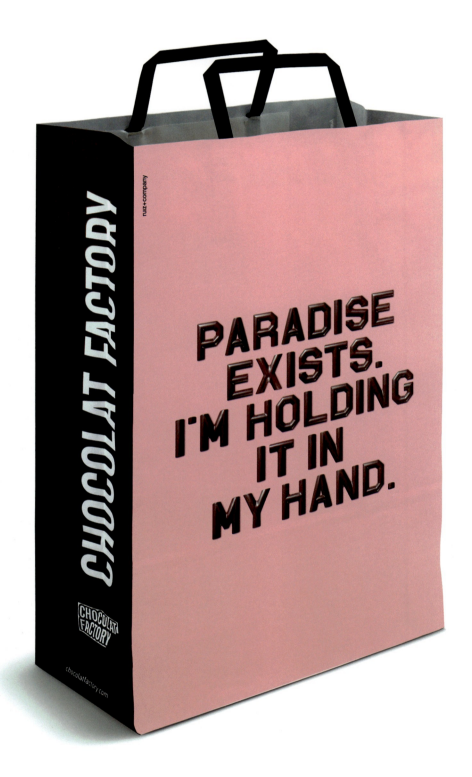

THE GILDED CAGE
DESIRE WRAPPED UP

GLAMOROUS PACKAGING relies on strategic and alternating uses of transparency and opacity, opulence and discretion, invoking the impossible perfection and bittersweet fantasy of everything from the Hollywood ingénue to Tiffany jewels. Eyeshadows are dressed up with texture, faceted like gems or quilted like the lining of the jewel box of a Versailles courtesan. But the influence of glamour extends beyond gilded shopping bags, silk boxes and the marketing of eternal youth: it is key to gratuitous consumption in the liquor, fashion and jewellery industries as much as cosmetics, beauty and scents. Painting images of the lush life, this type of packaging exploits the aspirations, of those reaching beyond the status quo, as much as it exploits the wealth – of those striving to maintain their status.

"People buy luxury products based on product and brand reputation and less on shelf presence," says Lovely Package founder and editor Chris Zawada. "But no one wants to buy a $200 bottle of perfume that comes in some generic off-the-shelf bottle and a raw cardboard box." Happily, big production budgets allow designers of luxe packaging to experiment extensively with unique solutions, materials and printing techniques. The Arnell Group's 1000 Acres vodka bottles are a tribute to bespoke glass manufacturing and simple materials: clear glass, white porcelain, cork – time-honoured materials unspoiled by text or logos. The sculptural shape of the four different bottles defines the product. Each is tall and slender with all but one made from glass: a rectangular glass box stoppered with a long cork set at a jaunty angle; a gently wasp-waisted cylinder with an exaggerated punt and a thermos-like lid; a refinement of the double-handle amphora; and finally an opaque porcelain bottle with willowy appendages.

Sometimes opulence is indicated energetically through type, metallic and jewel tones, lush colours and plush materials; at other times, austerity is the symbol of quality. For lingerie label Kiki de Montparnasse, TK Designer made shopping bags with sans serif logos on a matte black ground, as simple as a velvet rope, designed to stimulate, so to speak, the curiosity of a discriminating clientele. Packaging like this suggests that the product, beyond doubt an object of superior, even exclusive, quality, should remain the focus of the shopping experience (even if it sometimes piques interest precisely by not defining the character of the product).

In Berlin, Humiecki & Graef's Sebastian Fischenich and Tobias Mueksch have developed a fragrance line that achieves exactly this. Despite the obvious luxury of the scents, the bottles look ascetic, proud and reticent, rich without excess, soft spoken but expressive. "Our aim was to follow the design principle that big effects can be conjured even with small changes," says Fischenich. Individual flacons were created for each fragrance as if each bottle was a reliquary casket dedicated to the powerful persona of each partner's beloved grandmother – a vessel to safekeep emotions. The flasks' beribboned rectilinear shapes and caps echo the casket's right-angled form and the traditional cedulae stitched with the name of a saint. Colour and material play a crucial role in defining each fragrance: The cap for Geste, which evokes the love of an older woman for a younger man, is made of porcelain, a feminine material that is as fragile as it is strong since it is fired at very high temperatures. "The simplicity of the design should keep the focus on the most important thing, the fragrance," insists Fischenich. "A perfume flacon is just packaging, a 'reliquiar' for a very exceptional creation. This should be celebrated and not overcome by unnecessary design."

These product mosaics contain many of the Comme des Garçons perfume designs and show the kaleidoscopic diversity of their product lines which, nevertheless, retain a stylistic coherence. The common denominator in Atlan's CdG work is the preeminence given to typography and its unusual placement, the bold choice of concepts, and the level of attention bestowed on each detail. Atlan eschews marketing analysis and focus groups in favor of a deliberate pursuit of uniqueness. Precisely what the Comme des Garçons client is looking for.

MARC ATLAN

Product: Multiple Secondary Packaging
Client: Comme des Garçons
Material: Multiple techniques

Product: Samples and Gifts (gold, silver, copper)
Client: Comme des Garçons
Material: Vacuum-packed and silkscreened
glass, paper offset-printed with metallic inks

In this Comme des Garçons special samples set,
oversized plastic wrap incongruously dwarfs
the small perfume vials it contains. The scents
are nestled in a copper printed sheet. Precious
metallic colours stand in contrast to the functional
and technological aspect of these unpretentious
compositions. The large-scale fonts printed on the
background of the candle and eau de parfum gift
pack become distorted and are partly obscured
by the randomly placed encapsulated objects.
To underscore the gifts' one-of-a-kind nature,
the shrunken plastic crumples each metallic mini-
poster into a unique shape.

MASH

Product: Evo Product Cases
Client: Evo
Material: vintage cases, pink satin, foam

Mash created a product package that could hold a variety of Evo product sets. These valises are used by sales representatives when visiting potential and existing buyers. Mash sourced a variety of used vintage cases and then screen-printed their exteriors and customized the linings of the cases with pink satin to cushion each Evo product snugly.

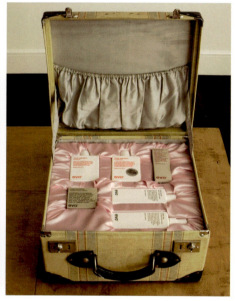

TURNER DUCKWORTH: LONDON & SAN FRANCISCO

Product: Christmas Gift Packs '06
Client: Liz Earle Co. Ltd.
Material: Extrusion blow-molded plastic bottle, injection moulded plastic cap and die-cut recycled paper labels

Duckworth's design solution for gift packaging took inspiration from the winter landscape and the feeling of anticipation of the approaching holiday season. As shoppers open the lid they reveal silhouetted trees against a snow-softened horizon.

**STEPHEN BURKS /
READYMADE PROJECTS**

Product: Missoni Profumi
Client: Estee Lauder / Missoni
Material: Missoni fabric, gradient painted glass, cast acrylic and printed gold foil carton

This collection of primary and secondary packaging was designed by Burks to incorporate original Missoni fabrics into every bottle. The extract is contained in a glass bottle completely "upholstered" in Missoni's signature chevron fabric, while each eau de toilette features a fabric collar over a gradient-tinted flacon. This means that no two bottles are ever alike. The boxes are dressed in the brand's signature reds, yellows and oranges over metallic gold foil.

HELVETICA INC

Product: Truffle Ice
Client: Hefti Jeunesse

DIZEL & SATE

Product: Bags, Boxes
Client: Svartensgaten 7

LEO BURNETT LISBOA

Product: Knuckle Bag
Client: ClothesinClosets
Material: Aluminium and Gmund
worldline paper ebony

We've created an unusual, highly crafted
bag that attracts attention outside the store
and promotes the ClothesinClosets sale.
It has real knuckle dusters for holders which
were carefully handcrafted in aluminium, as
this is a small boutique with handcrafted
clothes as well.

MADE THOUGHT

Product: Carrier Bag
Client: Palazzo Grassi

MADE THOUGHT

Product: Stella by
Stella McCartney
Client: Stella McCartney

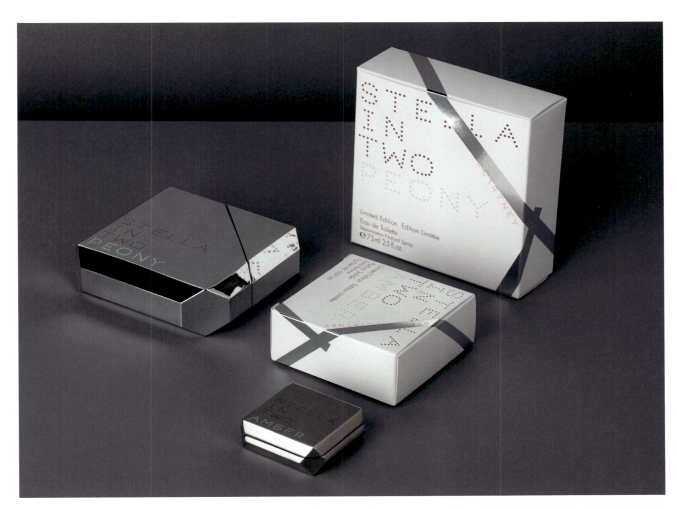

NORTH DESIGN

Product: Branding and
Packaging Design
Client: Princi

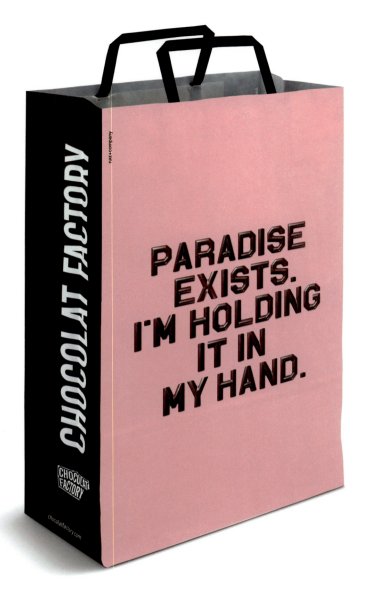

RUIZ+COMPANY

Product: Pleasure Experts Bags
Client: Chocolat Factory

This bag forms one part of a three-part series, each containing a different message about pleasure, which is the focus of the campaign.

Product: Poster
Client: Chocolat Factory

Product: Pocket Tubes
Client: Chocolat Factory
Material: Aluminium

These capsules hold various flavours of chocolate nibs to keep them close at hand, in a handbag or deep pocket.

Product: The Rain
Client: Chocolat Factory
Material: Aluminium

Product: African Stones
Client: Chocolat Factory
Material: Aluminium

Packaging aimed at chocoholics and others who dare to purchase and have on hand 3kg of the dark stuff.

TORU ITO

Product: Pack-Unpack
Material: Paper

Conceptual design work for the exhibition "Pack-Unpack".

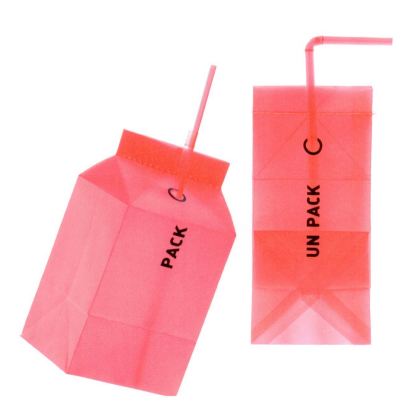

CAMILLA LILLIESKÖLD

Product: Very Important Products
Client: Habitat
Material: Corrugated cardboard printed in
high gloss

BVD

Product: Standard
and Gift Packaging
Client: Hennes &
Mauritz

STEPHEN BURKS / READYMADE PROJECTS

Product: CK IN2U Primary Packaging Prototypes and Study Models
Client: Coty Prestige/CK, Calvin Klein
Material: Polyester resin, polyethylene, rubber

Product: CK IN2U Primary Packaging
Client: Coty Prestige/CK, Calvin Klein
Material: Injection-moulded ABS plastic sleeve or skin over moulded glass bottle

This bottle shape combines traditional glass with an innovative injection-moulded plastic skin cut-thru containing the brand's logo. "A product, not a package," as the company says, the bottle compels shoppers to pick it up and turn it in order to read it. When launched, IN2U ranked number one in world fragrance sales forcing the factory to churn out a staggering million bottles per month to keep up with demand.

BEL EPOK

Product: Parfume Bottles
Client: Humiecki & Graef

MARC ATLAN

Product: Flameless Candle
Client: Helmut Lang
Material: Offset printing on labels, aluminium

CONTAINER LTD.

Product: Slingback
Material: PP

A result of Container's ongoing partnership with specialist cosmetics manufacturer HCP, the "Slingback" comes in both narrow and wide-body formats. The design allows for the use of the mirror when the compact is closed and is available in configurations of 4, 5 and 6 pans. The Slingback is one of a growing number of brands including Red Earth, Intercos and Sisley.

CONTAINER LTD.

Product: Original & Mineral Hair Care
Client: Original & Mineral
Material: PE

O&M are pioneers of ammonia-free colour technology. Container were commissioned to produce an identity and packaging that reflected the company's commitment to providing products free of harsh chemicals, containing ingredients that are pure, natural and nourishing. The styling products make a bold statement from the shelf when merchandised with O&M's other products. These bottles were designed to contrast playfully with the clean white lines of the shampoo and conditioner bottles. The colours and shapes target the slightly younger customer that buys the bulk of styling products. The bottle is round with a lozenge-shaped profile that references the caps on the wet products range and links the styling products to the rest of the range.

MADE THOUGHT

Product: Candle Packaging
Client: Yauatcha

DESIGNERS JOURNEY

Product: Olssøn & Barbieri 2009 Collection
Client: Olssøn & Barbieri
Material: Cardboard box and paper

Each bag is produced in no more than 50 numbered pieces a year, usually with minor revisions in between, which makes each product and collection unique. The cardboard boxes with their rigorous simplicity are thought of as totems and as an oath to hand-crafts rather than mere aesthetics, and the bags as product design rather than items following the pace of fashion design. Each bag also comes sealed, with a spot varnished tag, a short description, number and production year, completed by hand. The bags are made entirely by hand in Italy with the highest quality materials and craftsmanship.

BASE DESIGN

Product: Packaging
Client: Kiki de Montparnasse

CAMPBELL HAY

Product: Found Packaging
Client: Found Cosmetics
Material: Printed carton board, ceramic, plastic

Though minimal and understated, these boxes and tubs feature luxurious detail and a clean finish.

BASE DESIGN

Product: Ribbons, Ring Boxes, Bags
Client: Karen Karch

NURIT KONIAK

Product: Branding and Packaging
Client: Rhus Ovata

TORU ITO

Product: Metabolizer
Bottle and Pump Dispenser
Client: IPSA
Material: ABS, polypropylene, glass

SANDSTROM PARTNERS

Product: Alima Pure Makeup
Client: Alima Pure
Material: 100% recycled fibre paper board
(30% PCW)

Alima Pure makes mineral makeup using a minimum of ingredients. With the exception of a few boutique retailers, the only way to purchase Alima was through their website. In an effort to prove to their consumers that Alima's ingredients were pure and simple, the company voluntarily went through the painstaking process of gaining BDIH certification, a highly coveted European seal of approval for natural products. Today, Alima is one of only two U.S. cosmetics companies with BDIH approval. With the prospect of worldwide distribution, Alima hired Sandstrom to take the brand to a global level. The brand character was articulated through beauty tips emphasising inner beauty: "Smile. It reveals your inner beauty and makes you irresistible" and "Be impulsive. It adds colour to your cheeks and a twinkle to your eye." The tips became touch points for the company's packaging, collateral and website. The exterior packaging features illustrations by Amy Ruppel that are foil-stamped in pearlescent white on the natural cream stock. One exposed end of each box reveals the jars and product anchored by a simple sticker containing product information, which eliminates the need for extra runs and printing costs.

CONTAINER LTD.

Product: Körner Skincare Packaging
Client: Körner
Material: Polypropylene

This Körner jar uses a scallop detail to serve as a grip area for the lid. The thread inside the jar, which in traditional tubs usually fills with the cream or liquid over continued use, is deliberately hidden within the double-walled structure so that the jar always looks clean. The designers, however, give a glimpse of the internal structure which can be seen under the jar, which is suggestive of the technology used in the creation of the jar itself, as well as the formulations it holds. The unconventional structure of the tub reflects the brand's unconventional methods and acts as the "hero" of the product range.

Product: Kevin Murphy Hair Care
Client: Kevin Murphy
Material: High Density Polyethylene

"The building blocks of great hair" was the brand motto that helped shape all the Murphy packaging. When the company expanded to include a wet range, they introduced a slab-sided 250ml bottle. The cap is cantilevered from the base of the bottle, which has the virtue of keeping the product inside, perenially at the ready. A miniature version of the bottle has the same visual "voice", but at a lower volume.

Product: Kevin Murphy Hair Care
Client: Kevin Murphy
Material: Polypropylene

This jar is a single injection-moulded piece with a living hinge so that the lid can be flipped and locked. The one-material packing allows for an economy of manufacturing and easy recycling.

Product: Original & Mineral Hair Care
Client: Original & Mineral
Material: Polyethylene

These bottles express the brand philosophy. Reminiscent of a milk bottle, they connote purity, cleanliness and nourishment. The custom disc cap with its lozenge shape has become a signature of the brand.

MARC ATLAN

Product: Shower Gels
Client: Helmut Lang
Material: Silkscreened plastic jars

Product: Cologne Sample
Client: Helmut Lang
Material: Silkscreened plastic sleeve, glass, blind deboss on 5-ply cotton insert

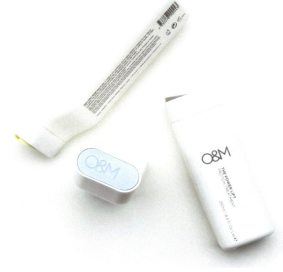

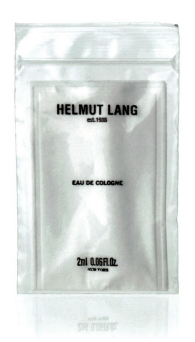

BASE DESIGN

Client: Kiki de Montparnasse

A luxury lifestyle shop specializing in lingerie and high-end sex accessories, Kiki de Montparnasse is named after the legendary muse of female empowerment. Base's identity for Kiki incorporates silhouettes of Kiki's products along with silhouetted illustrations of plants, animals, and mythological creatures associated with sexual power. These illustrations are arranged in a variety of patterns and compositions throughout the identity. The idea of the muse plays into Base's art direction of Kiki's image campaign, as well as copywriting, which centres around the line "Thinking of you thinking of me." Base's project for Kiki includes the logo, garment hangtags and product packaging, shopping bags, gift boxes, ribbon, stationery, a mailer and a catalogue. Base's work also informed and was integrated into the company's website (in a collaboration with Sweden Unlimited) and on various interior design elements for the shop (with interior design studio, Commune).

HOMEWORK

Client: Lust

CLOT INC.

Client: Clot & Nike
Material: Wood

The Nike Clot Air Force 1 comes in a special "Chinese Candy Box."
Traditionally, Lunar New Year celebrations include offerings of
sweets and other edible treats arranged in a red lacquer box to
ensure a "sweet" coming year. Honouring this custom, the CLOT
Nike Air Force 1 packaging comprises a hexagonal red box with a
partitioned tray layer to hold shoe accessories, and a matching lid.
The box exterior is adorned with CLOT graphics in black.

LAUREN GOLEMBIEWSKI

Client: SiO
Material: Paper

SiO is a jewelry store that specializes in glass and crystal jewellery.
The unusual faceted bag for the shop was designed in this mineral
shape in order to emphasize the way that light hits a crystal. This
formal gesture is repeated in the form of the logo and in a crystal-
line inner box that also features faceted sides.

HELVETICA INC

Product: Glamacy Fragrance
Client: Kanebo

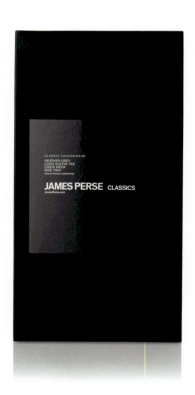

MARC ATLAN

Product: Versatile Loungewear Collection
Client: James Perse
Material: Offset printing on label and paper

MARC ATLAN

Product: Christmas Pillow
Client: Comme des Garçons
Material: Bead-filled black velvet pouch,
silkscreened tag

Every holiday season, Comme des Garçons
comes out with a limited-edition eau de parfum,
using the existing bottle but modifying its aspect
in some extravagant or unusual way. This time,
the scent was shrouded in plush black velvet,
with the intention of blurring the line between
fragrance and fashion. The woven label, containing
all product information, simulates a clothing tag.

MICHAEL FREIMUTH

<u>Product:</u> Azita's Almost-All-American Rubs
<u>Client:</u> Azita's
<u>Material:</u> Wood, aluminium

<u>Product:</u> Azita's Almost-All-American
Hot Sauce
<u>Client:</u> Azita's
<u>Material:</u> Moulded Plastic, aluminium

The namesake and Persian-American chef
of a Chicago-based cookshop, Azita commissioned these limited edition dry rubs as
a promotional gift for a shortlist of business
partners and investors. Produced using
sustainable materials, the packaging was
designed to match the minimal aesthetic
and playful typography that have become
signature elements of many of Azita's
products.

Product: Brand Identity and Packaging
Client: 826 Valencia Pirate Supply Store Products

THE NEW
OLD-FASHIONED

REAL, HANDCRAFTED and unrefined, Retro packaging makes use of vintage illustration and typography, handwritten labels and shapes that recall anything from the post-war brands of the 50s, 60s and 70s to mid-19th century dry goods stores with sawdust on the floor and burlap flour sacks. These packages use unfussy materials: matte cardboards, unbleached papers or natural fibres and solid, traditional materials like glass that imply a certain degree of purity and wholesomeness. Australian cosmeceuticals retailer Aesop bottles its creams and potions with shapes and sober colours that resemble old-fashioned pharmacy packaging. Toothpaste brands from the British Euthymol to Muji's generic come in squeezable aluminium tubes that resemble artist's oil paints from the mid-1800s.

Retro packages also appear to have been made with the meticulous attention usually reserved for an artisanal product, something we associate with an era in which deep personal expertise coexisted with naivete, before the hard sell became commonplace. They suggest a return to pre-industrial virtue, to a time when there was no choice but to make things by hand – and we were better for it. It is an aesthetic that is approachable, human-scale, and made, jarred, canned or bottled by humans instead of machines.

Most often, Retro labels stand out in cacophonous retail space and on crowded shelves because they "speak" softly instead of shouting, especially in contrast to today's ubiquitous and vociferous "traffic-light" packaging. These wrappers and labels feature iconic illustrations, cheerful, warm pastels and mid-tones set against more earnest black, brown or cream backgrounds. Minimal or simple repeated patterns are enlivened and updated with limited – perhaps, one or two – colours. Embellished, robust type with simple flourishes and serif lettering or handwriting declares that this is a longstanding heritage brand. Straight-talking and candid, it is a product of high quality and good value that is what it says it is and does precisely what it claims to do on the label.

Rick and Michael Mast of Mast Brothers Chocolate in Brooklyn originally wrapped their artisanal chocolate bars in butcher paper but switched to vintage patterned papers that they had either collected over time or discovered in New York Central Art Supply's second-floor paper room. "The traditional shape of the chocolate bar provides a nice foundation, allowing risks to be taken with the chocolate itself and with the wrapping concept," says Rick who recently commissioned graphic artist Mike Perry to design a label and curate a series of ten others by local artists. "We wanted every aspect of our bean-to-bar, artisan chocolate to be of the highest interest and integrity – while still having fun. Our techniques and philosophies are perhaps perceived as 'old-fashioned' but we are huge fans of new art and new ideas, particularly if they involve something done by hand, by someone we know."

ID BRANDING

<u>Product:</u> Lovejoy Vodka
<u>Client:</u> Integrity Spirits

PALATAL COLLECTIVE

<u>Product:</u> Bath Products
<u>Client:</u> Jonquille

SCHEIN BERLIN

<u>Product:</u> Cacao Liqueur
<u>Client:</u> Various movie industry productions

ZOO STUDIO

<u>Product:</u> Wedding Party Favors
<u>Client:</u> Ramon Morató / Salma Hayek
<u>Material:</u> Carton, glossy plastic

The floral motifs on the box evoke the frill of a wedding dress. It is a fine, geometric pattern in white on a metal silver ink background. A vegetable paper is used to protect the four chocolates inside the box, which includes a description, written in metal ink, of each chocolate in typography that reinforces the femininity of the pack.

CLARA EZCURRA / MARÍA OLASCOAGA

Product: Amalia Sparkling Wine
Client: Viña Amalia Winery
Material: Custom-shaped wine label paper,
hardboard tube, embroidered lace

EDWARD PEARSON

Product: Espiritu de Elqui
Client: Fundo Los Nichos
Material: Aluminium, black painted glass with
white screenprinted text, complex aluminium
alloy cap, flexo cardboard box

SHON TANNER

Product: Waffle Cone Packaging and Ice Cream Tubs
Client: Ticino ice cream
Material: Cardboard

COLLEEN MEYER / IMAGEHAUS

<u>Product:</u> Seed Bags
<u>Client:</u> All Seasons Wild Bird Store
<u>Material:</u> Brown Kraft paper

DESIGNERSJOURNEY

<u>Product:</u> Herregårdsgløgg
<u>Client:</u> Arcus As
<u>Material:</u> Clear-on-clear foil label

This clear label evinces the spices and scents that are the ingredients for this holiday beverage in an abstract way, while lightening and invigorating the bottle's presence on the shelf through the use of a clear-on-clear foil with a thick lacquer finish.

WILLIAMS MURRAY HAMM

<u>Product:</u> Chocolate Bar Wrappers
<u>Client:</u> Divine Chocolate

Hamm shifted the look and feel of the Ghanaian brand from a fair trade product to a premium chocolate of choice, without losing sight of its fair-minded credentials. The packaging uses local Adinkra symbols, which are indigenous to Ghana and the farmers who co-own the Divine company. The interlocking pattern these create and the use of gold foil in the hand-drawn logo convey a sense of luxury.

LOUISE FILI LTD

<u>Product:</u> Cookie Boxes
<u>Client:</u> Tate's Cookies

LOUISE FILI LTD

Product: Calea Nero d'Avola
Client: Polaner Selections

Influenced by Italian poster design of the early 20th century.

CLARA EZCURRA / MARÍA OLASCOAGA

Product: Viña Amalia Reservado
Client: Viña Amalia Winery
Material: Custom label paper, silk paper

PALATAL COLLECTIVE

Product: Bath Products
Client: Joie

BRAHM

Product: Loose-Leaf Tea Tins, Take-Away Cups, Bags
Client: Mallard

MAST BROTHERS CHOCOLATE

Product: Chocolate Packaging

Originally, Rick and Michael Mast wrapped their artisanal chocolate in butcher paper, but they were drawn to patterns and craved a little variety. At the New York Central Art Supply, they scavenged for vintage papers or used patterns that they had collected over time. Mast have also commissioned a series of original wrapper designs from Brooklyn artists that will be curated by graphic artist Mike Perry.

MUCCA DESIGN CORP.

Product: Sant Ambroeus Restaurant Boxes, Bags, Tins, Doilies
Client: Sant Ambroeus

The designers preserved the original logo of this traditional Milanese restaurant, using an historic type from the 1930s. Mucca also created two additional typefaces, one based on a period script printed on their illustrated wrapping paper, and one based on a sans serif typeface found on Art Deco-era food packaging. Since it opened, Sant Ambroeus had used a signature salmon colour that had a strong visual association to cakes and confections and had become deeply familiar to its customers. However, the colour had not been used consistently—the hue varied from item to item; Mucca standardized it on all printed materials to create a consistent look for the brand. In this way, by incorporating elements from the business' existing collateral, the team created an identity that is both fresh and founded in an esteemed company's legacy and reputation.

YAEL MILLER / MILLER CREATIVE

Product: Ciel Pur Signature Soap
Client: Ciel Pur
Material: SBS paperboard

A hand-assembled box made of textured folding paperboard with a removable tray that is drawn outwards via a decorative ribbon pull.

HERE DESIGN

Product: Cucumber Wrappers
Client: Hendrick's
Photography: Nick Turner

EYAL BAUMERT

Product: Zayde
Client: Zayde Liquor Company
Material: Fabric label

Zayde is an Israeli liquor brand whose character takes its cues from a "zayde", the Yiddish word for grandfather, a term commonly used in Eastern Europe. This persona is tastefully introduced through the use of labels in tweed and other fabrics.

ARUTZA ONZAGA / P576

Product: Mix-Your-Own Massage Oil
Client: Loto
Material: Amber glass

EYAL BAUMERT

Product: Zayde Wine
Client: Zayde Liquor Company
Material: The wine bottles are covered with paper which has a fabric trace on it.

SCOTT LARRITT

Product: Naturopathic Skincare
Client: Jacqueline Evans
Material: Amber glass, eyedroppers

The amber glass used for all the packaging not only preserves the integrity of the contents, it complements the restrained typography and distinct colours of the labels. The authenticity and quality of the product is communicated through a nostalgia-induced sense of trust.

KYLE POFF DESIGN

Product: Australian Blend Canadian Whiskey Bottle and Label
Client: Bull·A·Rook
Material: Glass, die-cut uncoated paper

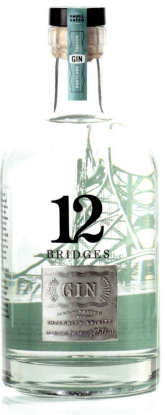

TODD LANDAKER / RED TETTEMER

Product: Tub Gin Bottles
Client: Tub Gin
Material: Glass bottle, cork stopper

Bottle design for small-batch gin.

ID BRANDING

Product: 12 Bridges Gin
Client: Integrity Spirits
Material: Glass bottle, cork stopper

Bottle design for small-batch gin.

FARMGATE

Product: The Glenrothes Scotch Whisky
Client: Berry Bros. & Rudd – Glenrothes

BRUICHLADDICH WHISKY

Product: Bruichladdich Whisky
The Yellow Submarine Special Bottling
Client: Bruichladdich

This label marks an event that occurred in the Hebrides' sleepy Port Ellen where a local fisherman found a mini-submarine with Ministry of Defence markings, bristling with state-of-the-art surveillance equipment.

Towed to port, the £500,000 spy kit was craned onto the fisherman's front lawn and the MOD alerted. First they denied it was theirs, then that it was missing and then accused him of stealing it. The fishermen refused to divulge its whereabouts. A stalemate ensued.

STAATAMSTERDAM

Product: Bols Genever
Client: Lucas Bols B.V.
Material: Glass bottle

The bottle takes its form from the shape of Bols' 19th century classic clay genever jugs but is executed in smoked glass instead of clay, to add freshness and sophistication. The traditional cork closure is preserved. The logo was inspired by the traditional Bols logo and Amsterdam's historical hand-painted café and shop window lettering. A calligraphic script was custom-made while the typeface used is an 18th century font derived from the Dutch Fell types, the Caslon.

MOR – INHOUSE DESIGN TEAM

Product: Nordica Freïa – Bath Essence Bottle
Client: MOR Cosmetics
Material: Ceramic, cork, cardboard, wood

This earthenware inspired ceramic bottle is designed for re-use and collection. Tied to the bottle are a wooden charm and a tag containing information about the product that doubles as a gift card because it contains an area reserved for a special handwritten message.

SANDSTROM PARTNERS

Product: Session Lager Bottle and 12-Pack
Client: Full Sail Brewing
Material: Metallic paper, corrugated paperboard

A pre-prohibition style American lager, Session comes in a stubby 11-ounce bottle with a retro-inspired label with the intention of appealing to a wider audience than the company's heavier ales. To save production costs, the carton is flexo-printed directly on white corrugated paperboard with engagingly asymmetrical wrap-around graphics in red, black and grey. Every panel is different.

OFFICE

Product: Brand Identity and Packaging
Client: 826 Valencia Pirate Supply Store Products

Office collaborated with 826 Valencia, a non-profit tutoring centre that sells pirate supplies in its store-front to draw kids into the free programmes held in the back. They helped reinvigorate the pirate supply store by developing a new identity and nearly 50 new products – inspired by the store's wildly imaginative, inspiring experience. All proceeds from the product sales benefit 826 Valencia's programmes.

AESTHETIC APPARATUS

<u>Product:</u> Tea Packaging
<u>Client:</u> Andrews & Dunham
<u>Material:</u> Tins, screenprinted, hand-applied labels

AESTHETIC APPARATUS

<u>Product:</u> Steve's House of Charm Le Petit Premiere Collection Haircare and Beauty Products
<u>Client:</u> Blue Q
<u>Material:</u> 18-point coated 2-sided stock with 4-colour printing, spot gold, emboss with a UV coat

The designers created a haircare and beauty brand (including packaging and shopping bag) for Blue Q that revolves around the story of a sweet but clueless, quasi-stylish, possibly closeted hair stylist named Steve and his "House of Charm" beauty parlour.

MOXIE SOZO

Product: Mints
Client: Newman's Own Organics
Material: Tins
Artwork: Pat Redman, Pat Creyts,
Teri Gosse

MITRE AGENCY

Product: Coffee Bags
Client: Krispy Kreme
Material: Recyclable plastic, lined bag with
resealable top

LOUISE FILI LTD

Product: El Paso Margarita Mix
Client: El Paso Chile Company

MOXIE SOZO

Product: Candy Packaging
Client: Red Dog Candy

MOXIE SOZO

Product: Salsa Packaging
Client: Fruta Del Diablo

MOXIE SOZO

Product: Candy Packaging
Client: Red Dog Candy
Art Director: Leif Steiner
Artwork: Pat Creyts

JULIAN ROBERTS / IRVING & CO

Product: Oat Digestives (Crackers)
Client: The Fine Cheese Co
Material: Carton

LOUISE FILI LTD

Product: Chili Spices Kitchen
Safety Matches
Client: El Paso Chile Company

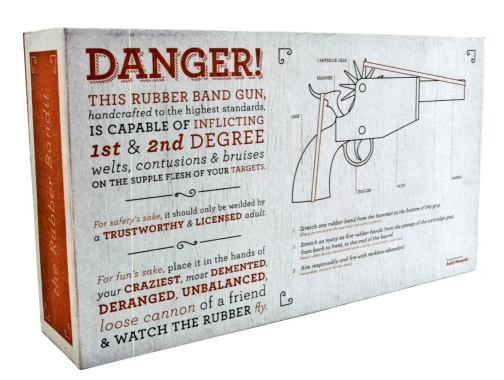

ANDY MANGOLD

Product: The Rubber Bandit
Client: Self-initiated
Material: Book board wrapped in inkjet-printed newsprint
form fitting die-cuts on the interior

MCLEAN DESIGN, INC.

<u>Product</u>: Havoline Motor Oil 100-Year Anniversary
Shipper / Display
<u>Client</u>: Chevron Havoline
<u>Material</u>: Kraft (unbleached) corrugated cardboard,
3-color post-print

BLEND-IT

<u>Product</u>: Caribbean Restaurant Bags
<u>Client</u>: Elephant

JOY D. CHO / OH JOY!

<u>Product</u>: Jelly Jar Candles
<u>Client</u>: Urban Outfitters
<u>Material</u>: Glass jar, metal lid, paper wrap

JULIAN ROBERTS / IRVING & CO

Product: English Fruits for Cheese
Client: The Fine Cheese Co
Material: Self-adhesive labels

JULIAN ROBERTS / IRVING & CO

Product: Natural Crackers
Client: The Fine Cheese Company
Material: Carton

Looking to the location of The Fine Cheese Company in the Georgian city of Bath, Irving created a modern but Georgian-inspired classic design to appeal to the widest swath of cheese connoisseurs.

MUCCA DESIGN CORP.

Product: Butterfield Market Packaging
Client: Butterfield Market
Material: Plastic

Mucca Design developed a visual language and style that naturally embodies the elegance and eclecticism of this market, its neighbourhood, and the New Yorkers who patronize it. Using the language of locals and locations ("Lex", "between 77th & 78th", and "NYC") became a tool that allowed Butterfield to highlight the shared cultural and geographic connection with its customers.

ARUTZA ONZAGA / P576

<u>Product:</u> Massage Oil Products
<u>Client:</u> Loto
<u>Material:</u> Recycled cardboard

A box made in recycled raw-looking cardboard conveys the purity and nature-oriented character of the product. On the other hand, the lithography and gold seal with curling serifs made in hot stamp lend an air of luxury to the box.

SUNHOUSE CREATIVE

<u>Product:</u> Aquapax
<u>Client:</u> Just Drinking Water Ltd.
<u>Material:</u> Cardboard

Aquapax is the only water in the UK packaged in an environmentally conscious carton rather than glass or PET. Rather than try and compensate for this with heavy-handed visual cues having to do with water, the demonstrative graphics emphasize the client's commitment to break away from category norms, take a stand for the environment and communicate a maverick, optimistic and premium feel.

CAMILLA LILLIESKÖLD

<u>Product:</u> Boots Original Beauty Formula
<u>Client:</u> Boots
<u>Material:</u> Debossed uncoated card

SIMON THORPE / BRAHM DESIGN

Product: We're Perfect With Cereals
Client: Teamwork at Brahm
Material: Glass

Standard UK milk bottles presented in an archetypal carrier with an embossed foil tag give an old fashioned feel to.

SIMON THORPE / BRAHM DESIGN

Product: Egg Packaging
Client: From Our Farms
Material: Standard cardboard egg carton

JAN SCHAWE

Product: Tea Packaging
Client: Mutterland

TURNER DUCKWORTH

Product: Breadsticks
Client: Waitrose Ltd.

Focussing on the Italian heritage of the range and striving to educate consumers about the difference between Grissini (an everyday snack) and Torinesi (a pre-dinner party nibble with olive oil), Turner Duckworth used actual size photography of the product against a distinctly rustic graphic background while announcing to shoppers what the product is in large type.

DESIGNKONTORET SILVER

Product: Food Products Identity
and Packaging
Client: Koberg Vilt

Koberg Vilt markets traditional food products
with new ingredients, including wild-boar
salami with chilli and deer sausage with Bur-
gundy, made from game that roams freely in
the woods around the Koberg estate. The high-
visibility orange of hunting clothes is coupled
with a classic oak-leaf graphic that makes the
products stand out at the deli counter.

JULIAN ROBERTS / IRVING & CO

Product: VINI Swing Tag Label
Client: Carluccio's
Material: CMYK printed, hand-illustrated typog-
raphy on uncoated heavyweight recycled card

JULIAN ROBERTS / IRVING & CO

Product: Amaretti
Client: Carluccio's
Material: Carton

LOUISE FILI LTD

Product: Scorch the Porch Products
Client: El Paso Chile Company

KRISTINA SACCI

Product: Askinosie Chocolate
San Jose Del Tambo Ecuador Nibble Bar 70%
Client: Askinosie
Material: String repurposed from bags of cacao
beans, rubber band, cardboard canister

KRISTINA SACCI

Product: Askinosie Chocolate –
C-Ration Month Supply of Chocolate
Client: Askinosie
Material: Birchwood box

This box holds enough chocolate for three
squares a day plus four extras for emergencies.

**JULIAN ROBERTS & LUCIA GAGGIOTTI /
IRVING & CO**

Product: Panettone
Client: Carluccio's
Material: Cardboard carton, ribbon

The designers printed a silver foil pattern inspired by
Italian fireworks printed on vibrantly colourful backgrounds
to create a box able to hold its own on shelves.

JULIAN ROBERTS / IRVING & CO

Product: Panettone al Cappuccino
Client: Carluccio's
Material: Carton, ribbon

Roberts hand made a collage of typography
from found letters and Italian ephemera to
decorate this cake box.

MILLER CREATIVE

Product: The Painted Pretzel Label
Client: The Painted Pretzel
Material: Acetate plastic, paperboard caps, Strathmore labels, letterpress printing

Clear acetate tubes with chocolate-brown paperboard caps on both ends are labelled with letterpress-printed graphics anchored to the containers with smaller letterpress "seals" to keep the containers tamper-evident.

JULIAN ROBERTS & PRISCILLA CARLUCCIO / IRVING & CO.

Product: Balsamic Vinegar Range
Client: Carluccio's
Material: Flexigraph printing, self-adhesive labels, carton

MEDEA-DESIGN / HUBERTUS DESIGN

Product: Packaging for Macarons
Client: Péclard Zurich
Material: Carton, paper covering

High quality carton box with gold foil logo print on paper covering.

CHELSEA KOORNICK

Product: Vegan Cookie Dough
Client: Eat Pastry
Material: Hard plastic tub, paper label

The label of this hard plastic pint container has a wholesome retro appearance. Different colour schemes correspond to different dough flavors.

JESSICA KEINTZ AND ROSS BRUGGINK

Product: Rise 'n' Shiner Coffee (Concept Packaging)
Client: Equal Exchange and the Minnesota Roller Girls

STUDIO BOMBA

Product: Rewind Coffee, Tea & Cocoa
Client: Rewind Retrospective
Material: Foil coffee pouches housed in ABS plastic canisters

Designed for maximum retro-kitsch kitchen appeal whilst providing optimum storage conditions for Rewind's premium coffee, the canisters are food-safe, light-safe and steady-stackable in mix-and-match vintage colours, with a lid that seals just right, allowing the coffee to breathe but not sweat and which won't dislodge during the thermal shrink-wrapping process or transport.

MOXIE SOZO

Product: Cookie Dough Packaging
Client: EatPastry
Artwork: Charles Bloom

HATCH DESIGN

Product: Chocolate Package Design
Client: Charles Chocolate
Material: Canister, paper wrapper

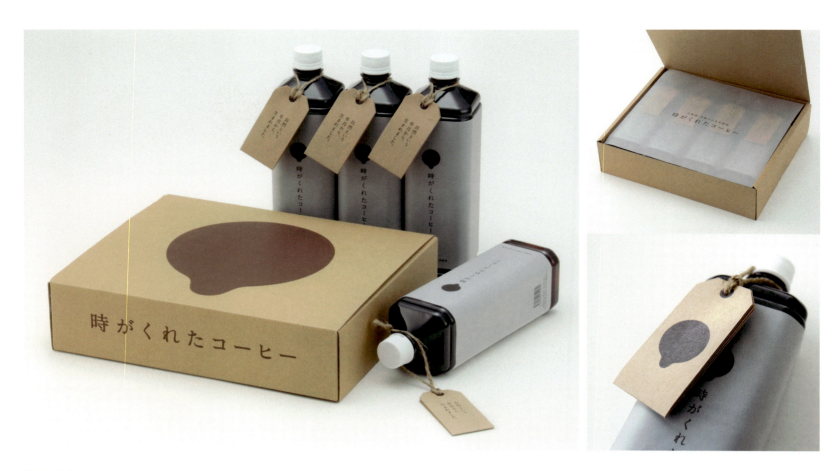

RYO UEDA

Product: Toki Ga Kureta Coffee
Client: Infini coffee

ERIC HOFFMAN

Product: Honey Sample Set
Client: Bee Raw Honey
Material: Scientific-grade glass, synthetic cork stoppers, beeswax, American oak block

Hoffman sealed nine individual glass vials with synthetic stoppers and beeswax and presents them in an American oak block and an E-flute carton with an illustrated raw brown paper insert.

ZOO STUDIO

Product: Code Egg
Client: Rubén Álvarez
Material: Rigid carton, adhesive paper

To pack the 'code egg,' a laser-cut corrugated carton was used together with an adhesive label giving the product a homemade, domestic look. The label is an adhesive paper designed to look like a typical store receipt while the tins resemble paint gallons. Code Egg is an exclusive product made in a limited series but the packaging design makes the product feel accessible. The box contains a black chocolate egg painted with cocoa butter and white alimentary colouring to mimick a real egg in colour, texture and shelf life.

LE LABO FRAGRANCES

Product: Candle Wholesale
Client: Le Labo
Material: Cross-cut kraft and stonewashed tin can

LE LABO AND
OIVIER PASCALIE DESIGN

Product: Fragrance Line
Client: Le Labo

HATCH DESIGN

Product: Wine Branding and Packaging
Client: Jaqk Cellars

HATCH DESIGN

Product: Wine Shippers
Client: Jaqk Cellars

MASH

Product: Return of the Living Red Wine
Client: Redheads Studio
Material: Fasson Estate 8 (label paper stock),
Spicers Stephen (envelope and card stock)

The 'Return of the Living Red' wine is labelled and packaged to echo its non-vintage character (because its two grape varieties come from different vintages, it is considered "ageless.") This quality lends the wine a certain mystery and intrigue which Mash amplified and visualized by creating a small pack containing missing or suppressed crime files, implying the existence of the living dead in and around the vineyards. These fictional dossiers contain disturbing anatomical illustrations and old photos on a toothy uncoated paper. A slip-knot with old twine and a deep red wax-dipped bottle deepen the atmostphere created by the old crime file.

216 \

SANDSTROM PARTNERS

Product: The Cost Vineyards Wine Labels
Client: The Cost Vineyards
Material: Digitally printed paper labels

The Cost Vineyards produces only 350 cases of Willamette Valley Pinot Noir, a renowned Oregon wine. Sandstrom created a different label for each bottle in a case of 12 bottles, using digital printing. Each label appears to be a clipping from a section of a fictional local newspaper. One is from the front page, another from the advice column, another from the classified ads and so on. Somewhere in the clipping, a mention of the wine appears and is encircled or underlined with pen.

SANDSTROM PARTNERS

Product: St-Germain Liqueur
Client: Cooper Spirits

MASH

Product: First Drop Wines
Client: First Drop Wines
Material: Fasson Estate 8 label paper stock

INDEX

BOXED AND LABELLED

NEW APPROACHES TO PACKAGING DESIGN

Edited by Robert Klanten, Sven Ehmann, Hans Baltzer
and Shonquis Moreno
Text by Shonquis Moreno

Cover by Hans Baltzer and Floyd Schulze for Gestalten
Cover motif "Milk Cocktail by Joe" by Hattomonkey
Layout by Hans Baltzer and Floyd Schulze for Gestalten
Typefaces: Planeta by Dani Klauser,
Foundry: www.gestalten.com/fonts,
Avenir by Adrian Frutiger
Foundry: www.linotype.com

Project Management by Julian Sorge for Gestalten
Production Management by Janine Milstrey and
Vinzenz Geppert for Gestalten
Proofreading by Patrick Sheehan
Printed by SIA Livonia Print, Riga
Made in Europe

Published by Gestalten, Berlin 2009
ISBN 978-3-89955-252-2

© Die Gestalten Verlag GmbH & Co. KG, Berlin 2009
All rights reserved. No part of this publication may be reproduced
or transmitted in any form or by any means, electronic or mechani-
cal, including photocopy or any storage and retrieval system, without
permission in writing from the publisher.

Respect copyrights, encourage creativity!

For more information, please check www.gestalten.com

Bibliographic information published by the Deutsche
Nationalbibliothek.
The Deutsche Nationalbibliothek lists this publication in
the Deutsche Nationalbibliografie;
detailed bibliographic data is available on the internet
at http://dnb.d-nb.de.

This book was printed according to the internationally
accepted FSC standards for environmental protection,
which specify requirements for an environmental management system.

Mixed Sources
Product group from well-managed
forests and other controlled sources
www.fsc.org Cert no. SW-COC-002883
© 1996 Forest Stewardship Council

Gestalten is a climate neutral company and so are our
products. We collaborate with the non-profit carbon
offset provider myclimate (www.myclimate.org) to
neutralise the company's carbon footprint produced
through our worldwide business activities by investing
in projects that reduce CO_2 emissions (www.gestalten.
com/myclimate).